Government Anarchy and the POGONOGO Alternative

THEODORE BECKER

Government. Anarchy. Two concepts that in the abstract are as incompatible as oil and water. After all, government is instituted to make, enforce, and adjudicate the law—in short, to counteract anarchy.

In fact, however, government has a great deal of trouble with anarchy, more trouble with anarchy in its own ranks than with anarchy outside it. Who guards the guardians? Who watches the watchdogs? When those who are there to uphold the law are the same ones who break it, what's to be done?

From the cop on the beat to the man in the White House, government is vulnerable to the menace of anarchy. According to Theodore Becker, it can scarcely be avoided. It isn't a matter of politics, of Democrats or Republicans; it's just that government officials, whether they are appointed or elected, seem to feel they are outside—or above—the law.

Official lawlessness happens most often because people in government can cloak themselves in privilege, red tape, the flag—and the

(continued on Back Flap)

p)

ently unshakable belief
re truly of, by, and for

that faith is shaken, as
ecent years? Throwing
eplace them with other
o have worked. Mr.
ONOGO Alternative:
government whose sole
watchdogs. With the
Anarchy Law and the
gative Ortho-Govern-
sure that every Ameri-
uld be coming to him

mother was fond of
es, " 'They laughed at

fessor of political sci-
Hawaii, is co-author of
in America. His light
chy?, has been shown
Circus, and will be on
campuses during the

Government Anarchy and the POGONOGO Alternative

THEODORE BECKER

STEIN AND DAY/*Publishers*/New York

Copyright © 1972 by Theodore Becker
Library of Congress Catalog Card No. 72-187545
All rights reserved
Published simultaneously in Canada by Saunders of Toronto, Ltd.
Designed by David Miller
Printed in the United States of America
Stein and Day/*Publishers*/7 East 48 Street, New York, N.Y. 10017
ISBN 0-8128-1461-4

The lines from *Loot* by Joe Orton are reprinted by permission of Grove
Press, Inc. Copyright © 1967 by Joe Orton.

This book is fully dedicated.

Contents

I

Government Anarchy—
Not Just Another Problem

The weed of crime
bears bitter fruit . . .
    —*Lamont Cranston*

Crime is contagious. If the government becomes a lawbreaker, it
breeds contempt for law; it invites every man to become a law
unto himself; it invites anarchy.
    —*Louis D. Brandeis*

Government anarchy probably began the first day the first official took office, an odd contention inasmuch as "officials" imply "government," and government and anarchy are held to be as compatible as Israelis and Arabs, or Montagues and Capulets. One can't have both in the same time-and-space warp. When one has government, one cannot have anarchy, and vice versa.

But since truth is relative, it frequently devastates our political definitions, which have a way of being absolute. As a matter of fact, degrees of government (control, order, etc.) and degrees of anarchy may well exist simultaneously. Furthermore, there can be degrees of anarchy within government itself. Such is true even in America.

Back in ancient Greece (where everything seems to have happened), government officials occasionally found it necessary to act above and beyond the law to achieve government goals they felt might elude them if they let their limited authority tie their hands. This is official anarchy, a breed of official lawlessness different from corruption or graft, where the official violates the law to increase his own personal fortunes. Ancient Greece had plenty of official corruption too, as well as its share of official incompetence.

All these problems in governance were pondered and discussed by the Greeks, but it remained for their philosophers to try to work out grand solutions, and to Plato in particular to philosophize a perfect state of government. His government was to be ruled by philosopher-kings (the conceptual ancestors of the White House staff), who would refrain from official anarchy and official corruption, and be incapable of incompetence.

But men of means and mind have been persistently skeptical

of Plato's solutions, and continue to raise the question so skill-fully dodged by the master: Who will guard the guardians? Who will keep the rulers within their allotted powers? For philoso-pher-kings, whatever their aptitude, will still be human, no matter how humane. Thus people have long been concerned about government officials' exceeding their authority either in-tentionally or unintentionally. And quite rightly so.

Only recently, however, has the problem of American official anarchy come to be considered worth worrying about. The debut of official anarchy as a national issue came during and immedi-ately following the Democratic National Convention in Chicago in 1968. This doesn't mean that most Americans became aware of the spread of government lawlessness that year, or are alert to it even now. But during that fateful week in August, official anarchy first became network-television clear, and thus a na-tional political issue.

What became frightfully obvious was a collapse of law on Michigan Avenue, Chicago, U.S.A., and only the most pedigreed political ostriches declined to notice that the police were at least co-engineers of that calamity. What lent this revelation im-portance was that it weakened resistance to the idea that even American government officials might flagrantly violate the law, and with impunity—a notion which would probably have met a pall of silence in any college class in American government as late as 1967.

Since 1968, police excesses that would never have been seen as connected are readily recognized as cousins to police lawless-ness. It also becomes increasingly easy to link other notorious events to the idea of government lawlessness: for instance, the undeclared war in Vietnam; the deceptions that got us into that mess; the search-and-destroy missions of the National Guard at Kent State and other universities; the travesty of trials con-ducted by many progovernment judges; official resistance to court orders regarding desegregation; and the federal government's attempt to censor the *New York Times* in the Pentagon Papers caper. All have made it plausible to argue that arrogant violations of the law by government officials occur repeatedly throughout our land.

Now I am not simple-minded or single-purposed enough to suggest that the acquiescent majority, wherever they increase, nurse this viewpoint as their own. Noting that a number of Americans have been primed to think along these lines, I am thinking more of the "influentials" (as American political scientists call them), the vociferous minority with money who have, at least potentially, the power to challenge the status quo.

This book is meant to encourage them and all those others who look to them for guidance on matters such as these. For it would also be folly to think that it is only a fringe group who understands government lawlessness.

In late 1970, James Michener was at Kent State researching a book on the tragedy there. After talking almost exclusively with campus "radicals," he was invited to speak to a fraternity group. He welcomed the opportunity, believing it would be a change of pace. Michener came away shaking his head: "Hell, those fraternity boys were just as radical as the radicals." [1] Those fraternity boys are some of the future leaders of America.

In other words, I believe that a large segment of the elite, the near-elite, and the future elite has come to sense the problem of government lawlessness of late. It is being felt in the right places.

WHY "ANARCHY"?

I must confess that the concept I coined to designate lawlessness by government officers to further the performance of their duty ("government anarchy") smacks of gimmickry. I could have stuck with "official lawlessness" or "government lawlessness." But "anarchy" conveys more of what is happening, I think, than does "lawlessness" or "outlawry." Also, it has infinitely greater capacity to move people to do something about it, especially those who ideologically or compulsively flirt with notions of "law and order."

In political theory, anarchy refers to a systemless system. Reading anarchist theorists, I get the feeling they believe men can succeed in governing themselves without the apparatus we call government. That mechanism is dispensable because it serves primarily the selfish and banal interests of those employed in making the contraption work (Parkinson's Law), as well as the goals of plutocrats and meritocrats in the society who wish to maintain their own privileges and dominance.

For the anarchist, this holds as true for a nominal communistic society as for a phenomenal capitalistic one. Modern-day anarchists (Yippies, flippies, and hippies) are as quick to snigger at the possibility of the "withering away of the state" in the Soviet Union, China, or Cuba, as they are to hoot and hiss at Fourth of July oratory proclaiming the eternal verities of our Constitution.

What anarchists admire is the antithesis of "government of law and not of men." They seek self-rule of men without externally imposed law and its cumbersome equipment of promulgation and execution. They entertain different assumptions about the political nature of man, whether in the state of nature or in the state of Vermont. They believe that if men were left alone to make up their own rules as they went along, according to their own ideas of what's right, society would be better off.

I was particularly intrigued by a comment of an American chief of police after his experience as an observer at the Woodstock Rock Festival in the summer of 1969. Chief Joseph Kimble, who has since been banished from the Beverly Hills Police Department, was astonished that over four hundred thousand young people could overpopulate a small area under terribly adverse weather and space conditions and get along so well, producing negligible violence and minor friction.

At Woodstock nearly half a million persons managed to simulate an urban slum, yet perform all animal functions happily—despite the near-absence of visible police power. As a matter of fact, the uniform of the token police force there was a red blazer, with no badge of authority except the Woodstock symbol: a dove and a guitar. Kimble emerged with some fresh ideas on the possibility that multitudes of people could police themselves with little structure akin to that we call police departments.

Was the Woodstock Nation a group of people living in anarchy? Yes. It was a gathering of people in large numbers who were determined to act in concert without regard to stone tablets, yellowed parchments, or rigid rulebooks.

Might not this concept apply equally to large blocs of government officials determined to implement their own ideas, also without regard to written laws or existent structure? I think so. But to call this "lawlessness" gives no inkling of the extent of the practice and the systemlessness that characterizes it.

For one thing, anarchy need not imply the existence of a physical boundary. It can exist as islands of action in currents of time and holes in space. Anarchy, or clusters of it, need not be based on a prevailing philosophy of anarchy. That was not the case at Woodstock, nor is it the case with official anarchists.

Moreover, anarchy inheres in some societies more than in others. Some might say that a deep, rich strain of anarchy has coursed through American culture from the beginning. Thomas Jefferson's statement about governments which govern least governing best packs a healthy anarchistic wallop, and Henry David Thoreau's views on civil disobedience have reinforced this kind of native American antigovernmental sentiment through successive generations.

In fact, a good argument can be made that roots of anarchism grow in the attitudes of most ordinary Americans about government and society. The common American bias would have it that politics is the low road; politics is dirty; politics is something you wouldn't want your son to marry. Yet politics is the business of government, like it or not.

And let us not forget the distrust by many Americans of something called "the federal government." A mouth-watering suspicion of centralized power pervades America. Many people rejoice in evading and defying any rule emanating from any office or edifice associated with the government. This is at the root of the argument of states' rights and local power against federal agents muddling through affairs not properly their own.

In addition to this universe of attitudes (all strongly supportive of antigovernment actions by private citizens) there is another cluster of American attitudes against rules in general. Stemming from these resentments is the inclination to respect the man who can "get away with something" at the expense of "the system" or some organization. The only time someone loses face for such conduct is when he gets caught. But his loss of stature is for his stupidity, when he is not pitied for bad luck.

Such an attitude is tied to a certain self-righteousness and solipsistic individualism that has traditionally torn at the American character, for in addition to admiring lawmen, Americans have also sung praise of defiant ones: those who resist a system which oppresses basic rights. (This is hardly as true, as James Baldwin notes, when the defiance comes in blackface.)

The vigilante group (or the lynch mob) is heavily romanticized in American folklore. Of course, it is widely castigated, too, e.g., the Whiskey Rebellion, John Brown's Raid, and the Oxbow Incident. But the fact remains that it is frequently applauded, as long as the rebel, like Huck Finn, acts on a belief in some superior morality, or on "obvious" pragmatism, or against the stupidity of "the system." Jefferson's incantations in the Declaration of Independence are an anarchist's catechism.

What we must remember is that American government officials are first and foremost Americans. Their official role might call for obedience, if not subservience, to the law they swear to uphold. However, their American consciousness deems it acceptable to disobey that law and discard the legal demands of their official roles with a clear conscience. It is perfectly compatible with the American superego, which equates some lawbreaking with high virtue.

Although officials would be loath to describe their own illegal activities, done to further the responsibilities of office, as "anarchy," the overarching effect of these actions is decidedly so. Increasingly strong crosscurrents of official anarchy are making the mainstream of American government almost unnavigable these days, and it promises to get rougher.

Official anarchy is not a sometimes thing. It involves government activities across the board. It involves our police, our military, our prison officials, our bureaucracy, our courts, our prosecutors, our governors, and our legislators. It is cleverly camouflaged, solidly entrenched, and nearly impregnable—at least up to now.

IT HURTS MORE

Official anarchy is not only a pervasive flaw in the American art of governance, but a particularly dangerous one at that. The danger arises not so much from the sheer existence of a tremendous amount of official anarchy as from the insidious effect it has on the American psyche.

Even on a smoggy day, one can see an ancient aphorism chiseled over a main entry into the Los Angeles City Hall: "He that violates his oath profanes the divinity of faith itself." This impertinence by Cicero has relevance to the more lethal effects of official anarchy. It refers to the necessity of one's adherence to his own highest allegiance. If that be in religion, then violation of his oath of belief or fidelity profanes religion. If his faith be in a higher secular law, say, a compact between men and their government, then the violation of his oath of office profanes that higher compact.

The successful operation of a free government requires deep reciprocal trust between the rulers and the people. Each must have equal respect for that system within which they all dwell, and each must believe the other maintains a healthy respect for that system. If large numbers of private citizens lose faith in the basic laws, and act out their disregard to the detriment of many others, then that is a high degree of anarchy, and those in government are bound to get surly about it. When evidence mounts that many rulers regularly violate their oaths of office, the basic laws, a surly public mood is equally sure to follow.

In the middle and late 1960's, the phrase "credibility gap" was used to describe just such a deepening dark frame of mind among many Americans. Lyndon B. Johnson became a man untrusted by large numbers of his fellow citizens, a misfortune rendered especially traumatic because, as LBJ himself observed, he was the only President they had.

To make matters worse, pronouncements by his various Cabinet associates and aides were also met with mounting skepticism. The explosion of distrust was ignited mainly by the President's statements about Vietnam, but there were reverberations in other presidential policy areas as well.

This particular "credibility gap," however, was symptomatic of an even larger one, a growing disaffection between many Americans and their government in general. What was happening was that official statements of important policy rather than mere campaign promises were being considered outright lies, and the mass media were making this clearer to the public than ever before in American history. This led to even greater political cynicism, particularly among recent college graduates and college students. To their way of thinking, many oaths of office were being profaned. A whirlwind of faithlessness in government was being sown.

Although outward signs of it have been muted, their anguish remains today and continues to fester. It stems from the chasm between the high ideals of the American Dream and the glaring

18

factual inconsistencies with that vision. For many of our young citizenry the journey to American perfection has become a bad trip.

No system is anything more or less than an intimate affair between the words that express its goals and ideals and the actual pursuit of them. Any system can tolerate some discrepancies between its ideals and reality. When they are infrequent or due to error, minor adjustments can be made. When they happen consistently, a crisis in confidence arises on the "efficiency" or value of the system. And the future of any system is in greatest danger when the youth in that system find it hard to live with. Sometimes the talk turns to revolution.

That is where we are today. The Vietnam War, the mass-media explosion, and the education implosion have exposed American official anarchy as never before, further degrading the idealism necessary to make any society cohere. Even where officials are not embarrassed, they are embarrassing.

What is more, government anarchy can be seen as the starting point in a cycle of growing disorder. The intolerably high degree of unlawfulness and disorder within government is likely to generate continued public disturbances (as a response to them), which will be ruthlessly repressed by those rallying around the "law and order" banner. So government lawlessness itself becomes a key factor in the steady decay of the general social order.

Official anarchy is truly menacing to the American system, whereas private anarchy, practiced by those with no access to government authority or power, is a paper tiger. A few wild men in low places, lobbing bricks through plate-glass windows on Main Street, planting pipe bombs in vacant New York skyscrapers, blowing a few unpoliced police cars to smithereens, and printing obscenity, heresy, and false bravado in newspapers with minuscule circulation, are no imminent threat to a construct with the history and sensibility of the American Constitution. However, a few mild men in high places, able to activate the

19

unfathomable power of the American system, when they have decided they are above that system, can wreck the very foundation of its trust.

In other words, official anarchy hurts a lot more than unofficial anarchy because it is the most potent, choate, and sinister threat to our fundamental law and order. Attorney General Mitchell once said, "Nothing has a greater tendency to create lawlessness than the lawless methods of law enforcement." [2] That was *William,* not John, Mitchell, and the year was 1930. But it is no less valid today.

It took only a mild rash of incitements to riot before Congress made it a crime to cross state lines to make trouble. Congressmen are very sensitive to the shenanigans of rebels *outside* government. The big question is whether Congress has the integrity to become equally determined to crack down on rebels *inside* government.

THE POLITICAL ISSUE OF THE DAY AFTER TOMORROW

So official anarchy is another political problem, but it is not *just* another one. It is extraordinarily important. Why do I think official anarchy is so special? Because there are such irresistible pressures in America for all kinds of change—forward, backward, random, planned, political, social, and economic—coupled with deep anxieties and reservations about change. To some undifferentiating minds, the desire for change is quickly transformed into a passion for a specter called revolution for the hell of it or to the brink of it, if possible. Whether the appeal comes from the Jefferson Airplane or the Watts left, the password and thumbshake signify "Revolution!"

But the self-styled revolutionaries have no consensus on either where to go or what to do once they announce they got there. So they will get nowhere. They are doomed to become a rebellion, a revolution that never made it, though they have made heavy contributions in publicizing the issue of government anarchy.

But there are strong counterpressures emanating from the Always Right, overreaction to even the slightest scent of any change, social, political, or economic. But they have no consensus as to where we *were,* so they will never get "there" either.

Worse still, there are flurries of agitation from what Jules Feiffer calls our "radical middle." This last force is willing to clamp down iron hard on both the left and right, so fearful are they of disruption of their fancied peace of mind and the order of things secular. This could be the strongest countervailing force of all. A pernicious status-quoism.

So we are in the midst of a Grand Turmoil, one that shows signs of waxing and waning, but persisting and probably intensifying as time slogs on. In terms of policy, the pressures for change concern the physical, economic, and environmental health of our nation. In terms of government, official anarchy is the major problem: inherent in American society, with its strange coalition of private and public anarchism, exacerbated by the society's runaway development into a Technocracy Supreme.

But American official anarchy, which has slipped by as an isolated series of irritations up to now, can only be arrested once the diagnosis of its collective existence and acuteness is understood and accepted. It will also help if those most aware of this now will tolerate the grim truth that there is little chance for any glamorous, cathartic, and successful suprasystem change and will wait for a much larger number of people to become equally aware of the seriousness of the situation. There is sufficient time (but keep your fingers crossed).

I doubt that there will ever be a drastic alteration of our political system at some definite point of time (my definition of revolution). But I think that there can be a slow and steady transition to a vastly improved political system, once the excessive revolutionary (change-the-superstructure) energy dissipates, its fervor channeled into sharp radical infrastructure change, and the critical mass for change (the new counterelite) comes into its own. Paul Samuelson, our Nobel Prize-winning economist, estimates the number of this elite to be somewhere between 5 and 10 percent of the population.

The two main failures of the complainers so far are that they (I am one) have not worked effectively to educate those on the verge of understanding the unhappy reality, and, more importantly, they (myself included) have scarcely begun to think hard at reasonable, rational, nonideological variations in our laws and political institutions, particularly to the point of altering the entire American constitutional arrangement.

To rebuff the push to the rear and resist punitive stand·patism, we have to offer far better than the romantic illusions of past thinkers in alien cultures. What's so radical about being a Trotskyite in 1972, even if Trotsky now looks like Richard Burton?

Government anarchy has been, continues to be, and forebodes to be a worse subversion and perversion of much of our established legal order than any other anarchies, fancied or practiced. We don't need to destroy our system. We need to resurrect and salvage it, yes, even "liberate" it, from our own government officials.

The American political system, if officially honored in practice, could be a far more effective instrument for change than it has ever been. But this must be made clearer to larger segments of the population, to accelerate the growth of the critical mass necessary to effectuate change.

If we do not work to rescue our government from official clutches, we stand an excellent chance of becoming subservient to a government entity responsible and valuable only to itself—which would also be a change, but for the worse. We do not need a new Constitution to do that, but we certainly need a better one. We need a mass infiltration into government by the enlightened. We need a lot of original thinking to strengthen it, and a new mobilization to implement it. That is the key challenge to re-creating the government of tomorrow.

Some people have already given substantial thought to solving some problems of government anarchy. But where the ideas have been unique and original to the American problem, they have also been piecemeal. That is because few have diagnosed the malaise as systemic, that is, shot through the body politic. To try curing cancer of the liver without realizing the patient has Hodgkin's disease is bad medicine.

Unfortunately, those very few who do see the general nature of the problem have been locked into ideological explanations (Marxism) and remedies (revolution). They got nowhere in America in the thirties and forties, and show even less spirit today. What is needed is some comprehensive streamlined scheme to bring official anarchy to heel. The solution I have to offer in this book is neither revamped Marxism, misplaced Maoism, nor displaced Taoism. Each has had its place in time. None can help us here and now.

So this book has several aims. First, it is an attempt to raise the level of public awareness of the fact that government has become one of the most dangerous single factions in our society. Many high and low officials are drunk with delusions of superiority to us in the rank-and-file citizenry. I shall briefly sketch how it shows.

Second, I hope to demonstrate, through several chapters, the many types and the high degree of official anarchy that prosper in our present system. The reader may well be aware of a number of the specific instances, but I suspect that few of those most aware have viewed the wholly ugly pastiche. Seen in its entirety, I truly hope it might move each reader to deeper and more concerned thought about temporary and final solutions.

Third, I should like to discuss some solutions already being tried and some I'm certain will be raised for future consideration. The penultimate chapter will treat some of the best of them

—and, I hope, dispose of them once and for all. For the chief goal of this book is to guide, ever constructively, the tender shoots of our growing antiestablishmentarianism. The political events and political personalities of today are helpless, considering inertia, to do anything but nourish this growing disestablishment over the years.

The final chapter is my proposal for radical political change. The strategy is radical political education. What we need is POGONOGO. And we need it badly. But more on that as we proceed.

2

The Most Dangerous Faction

Let them eat cake.
—*Marie Antoinette*

Once you've seen one slum,
you've seen them all.
—*Spiro Agnew*

The problem we are treating is not entirely new to American political philosophy or to American politics. Containing official authority was, as a matter of fact, the very first important governmental issue that our founding elite faced.

Thomas Jefferson was the most famous resister of centralized governmental authority. He had a number of reservations about "that document" emanating from the secret conclave in Philadelphia in the late 1780's. The delegates to that meeting, who had been empowered only to revise the old Articles of Confederation, produced a spanking-new document, explicitly allotting the central government vast new powers and explicitly mentioning only a few individual liberties (like *habeas corpus*).

Jefferson was outspoken in his opposition to the new Constitution. Many others entertained a deep-seated mistrust of such a powerful national government, and the Federalist Papers were an elaborate response to allay these fears. One of the best-known Federalist Papers, Number 10, dealt chiefly with limiting the power of the proposed new government.

In this document, James Madison conceded that many "considerate and virtuous citizens" were alarmed at the art of government in America and were skeptical about some of the solutions being propounded, including much of the recommended Constitution. Madison agreed that anxieties about a strong government were not groundless; he realized, too, that there was "increasing distrust of public engagements, and alarm for private rights, which are echoed from one end of the continent to the other." The source of this anxiety, according to Madison, was "factions," which he defined as:

27

a number of citizens, whether amounting to a majority or minority of the whole, who are united and actuated by some common impulse of passion, or of interest, adverse to the rights of other citizens, or to the permanent and aggregate interests of the community.

Madison believed that factions were inevitable in all societies because of the nature of man himself. Different capabilities, perceptions, and circumstances pit man against man, and make him seek allies. The mutual-interest groups that then form (factions) are inflamed with "mutual animosity" and are even prone to violent conflict.

Government's function is to regulate these contests before violence ensues. But because factions try to win control of government, government necessarily becomes involved with "the spirit of party and faction." At the same time, government must not take sides or it will fail to act in the public interest. What can be done?

The last thing to be done, according to Madison, is to expedite the goals of factions with respect to their gaining control of government. Factions must have as little liberty as possible, for, as Madison puts it, "Liberty is to faction what air is to fire." Steps must be taken to lessen the freedom of factions to act as they please.

Federalist 10 is essentially an argument for the principle of separation of powers. As Madison notes, the causes of faction cannot be removed (as they inhere in man), so their effects must be. The best way of preventing any faction from gaining a monopoly of governmental power is to divide up the powers, making it far more difficult for any single faction to overwhelm the government.

Federalist 10 was an appeal for a *federal* separation of powers as a superior way to deter factions (even when they constitute a majority) from forcing their will. Federalist 51 argued that separation of powers among branches would keep a government free of control by factions. Government had to be carved up in order to keep interest groups from capturing its tremendous powers and putting them to their own personal use. As Madison put it, no single faction should be able to control the reins of government, which is to mediate all interests. "No man is allowed to be a judge in his own cause, because his interest would certainly bias his judgment, and, not improbably, corrupt his integrity."

What the Federalist authors neglected to emphasize was that *government can become a faction itself!* Those who occupy the many levels and agencies of the government apparatus have a set of interests peculiar to themselves that are alien, if not hostile, to those outside government. Although our government of the people, by the people, and for the people remains that, it is fast turning into a government of the government, for the government, and by the government as well.

This is not just another way to say that power corrupts. It is to say that being in government can create a sense of being other than "of the people." It is to say that being a government official gives a sense of being above the law and a sense of being more important as a person, a sense that rarely exists among those out of government.

Those in government authority have a tendency to identify themselves with the state, which is above mere mortals. So when they act in an official capacity, their actions are suprapersonal—and they treat others as lesser souls. It is like the phenomenon of sales personnel in fancy shops or waiters in *haute cuisine* restaurants: they assume the snobbishness they believe to be worthy of their superiors. But in restaurant and boutique businesses it is the clientele who are the superiors. In government, the chiefs are superior, the clientele ("We the People") are the inferiors.

Important people and wealthy people in private life have been known to seek governmental positions in part because of this sense of individual transcendence which seems to inhere in government office. Why else do the Rockefellers, Harrimans, and

Kennedys seek high posts? It is not for money, and not for power, and not for deference. They have plenty of all that. And it is surely not *all* from a sense of altruism and public service (though there may be some of that). No, even lesser officials develop a sense of suprapersonal superiority to others, a sense that carries over to their private associations.

SURVIVAL AT OUR EXPENSE

I don't mean this holds true among all government personnel; it probably holds most true at higher levels of government, and among many of those who enjoy the monopoly of authorized physical force. How else can one explain the fact that the governments of the U.S.A. and U.S.S.R. from time to time seriously contemplate an agreement to limit antiballistic missile deployment to two cities, Washington and Moscow? Why should Washington or Moscow be spared nuclear obliteration? Should the governments of America and the Soviet Union decide to wage a thermonuclear war, they will have failed us all. Washington and Moscow should be the first cities to go, not the only ones spared.

As a matter of fact, it has long troubled me that our corporate leaders (political and quasi-political) have anesthetized themselves from the throbbing fear of split-instant atomization, should they stumble us all into an insensate "thermonuclear exchange" (as some quaintly put it).

Naturally the rationale follows that in the event the war is "thrust upon us" (ha!), there is *need* for continued operation of government. Let's all wonder aloud about that. But let's *worry* about whether these same men, as it has been stage-whispered, have provided their immediate kin with the keys to this underground kingdom of bunkers.

That bothers me. For why should I, a dues-paying citizen, finance such personal safety and family benefits for my so-called "public servants" if they flub their primary mission—to protect me, as well as us all, from externally originated obliteration? It makes no sense to me personally and it makes nonsense to me in terms of prerestructuring a postholocaust America. Why would we want that new leadership to be comprised of old leaders who were such dreadful flops? Such a governmentally set set of priorities—of who should survive—is explicable only when we realize how important those who rule us think *they,* and *their personal interests,* are, at our expense, tax and otherwise.

If they were truly *public* in their outlook and leadership, they would consider another set of priorities and would ask *us,* the society, to at least participate in establishing the kind of leadership and representation to emerge from our very own ruins.

Do we need double trouble in the rubble? Since we are paying for these heavenly subterranean havens, it is we who should decide who will populate them. Do we need a top-heavy bunch of bureaucrats, generals, and technicians to crawl out and start another "affluent society"? Or do we want more (some!) poets, artists, artisans, and the like, to try to reach for the moon here on earth, to grasp at Huxley's Pala, instead of another Brave New World?

Furthermore, if our leaders were truly that, dedicated to *public* service and the well-being of this entire society (as they say they are), then we might expect them to hold themselves (if not their families) hostage to any such atomic-hydrogen pyrotechnics. If their theory of mutual deterrence is invalid, it is only just that their families should join the vast majority of the rest of us. It would be a sort of domestically inspired deterrence as well.

I have nothing against these men or their families. I'm just trying to point out how these men conceive of themselves, as officials, as being over, better, or more important than us underlings, the great unwashed. But as thinkers, they show little promise. For in the event they should have to go under, then they would have proved that they were probably *worse* than the rest of us, since none of us could ever err so tragically.

"MAYDAY! MAYDAY!"

The turn of events in the spring of 1971 furnished two astounding instances of how government proved that it considered its own interests far more important than legally established private rights. The first of these was the Mayday arrests in the District of Columbia (with the Nixon administration's endorsements and eulogies); the second was the attempted suppression of the *New York Times'* and other newspapers' disclosures of the Pentagon Papers. These episodes drew banner headlines throughout America, and were splendid illustrations of government anarchy in action. Quite possibly they are even better examples of how government has become a faction unto itself, far beyond the pale of our law.

The Mayday arrest of some twelve thousand people in the District of Columbia was local police lawlessness *in extremis*—this despite the fact that D.C. police chief Jerry Wilson is one of the more reasonable men to occupy a top cop position in America. During the November 1969 Moratorium, the Washington police were, by and large, models of decorum. Chief Wilson's notions of police limits are quite exemplary. But he has a few notable blind spots, and one of them concerns acceptable police responses to intentionally disruptive tactics by political activists. One might say his views made the D.C. police prone to over-reaction, illegal overreaction.

When I interviewed him in late December, shortly after the 1969 Moratorium, I asked him to justify the heavy use of tear gas around the Justice Department, when the Yippies broke windows and threatened to batter down the front doors of that building. Wilson's argument went as follows: If he didn't stop them from "trashing" windows, they would have tried to break down the front door. If they tried to break down the front door, and succeeded, they would have broken into the building. If they got that far, they might have broken into offices and started to break up furniture, loot cabinets, and perhaps urinate on the floor. I asked him what he would have done in that event. His reply was, calmly and simply, "We would've had to kill them."

That statement did not come as any shock to me. After all, in 1968, Mayor Daley's order to the Chicago police to shoot to kill and maim looters occasioned little public outrage. Yet Daley's Manifesto was a perfect example of how high government officials think they are above the law—and one comes to expect this from others at similarly high levels.

Our law provides that capital punishment be limited to a very few kinds of grave offenses against the person, like murder. Neither the federal government nor the laws of any state provide the death penalty for stealing, burning, or destruction of real or personal property or for public lewdness. Yet Mayor Daley and Chief Wilson manifested no public compunctions about their willingness to have police murder people who were destroying or stealing property alone.

Why are the lives of policemen so much more important to policemen and other officials than the lives of mere citizens? Clouds of tear gas and extensive lawful arrests, with consequent legal punishments, are deterrents well within the legal bounds of American criminology and penology. Yet when highly entrenched officials rate government property above life, and daily bureaucratic functioning above the call of lawful law enforcement, Mayday's kind of government anarchy can hardly come as a surprise.

The grimmest part of the Mayday arrests was that the President of the United States publicly condoned widespread illegality by the police in order to keep government plodding for the day. Indeed, the mere threat that some American citizens were determined to violate traffic and property laws in order to slow down or shut down some governmental operations for a day, or two, or three, was enough reason to encourage police unlawfulness to prevent it.

There can be no question that the police and the federal government have the right and duty to protect themselves against such a menace to their routines and that they have the right and duty to enforce applicable laws on the books. A partial governmental shutdown was possible at the hands of large numbers of lawbreaking people, and this made the situation tense and difficult for the police. But that in no way justified the obviously illegal behavior the police indulged in for several days.

The extent of this illegal police behavior was made clear by the many thousands of cases that were subsequently dismissed. The police conducted dragnet arrests in certain areas of anyone who appeared to them to be a radical-type student or sympathizer. This tactic cleared the streets of potential believers in civil disobedience and filled the ugly compounds set up to imprison them. It also lined the streets with large numbers of blue-uniformed anarchists intent on shredding the legally protected social fabric of the whole community just to keep government running.

Is it better to break the law to keep government running than to allow others to break the law to stop it? Are traffic laws more important to policemen than the Bill of Rights? The clear implication is that to government officials, governmental operations are more beyond the law than private interests, in spite of the fact that government officials have a greater, in fact, a sworn, duty to follow law.

THE *TIMES* WAS RIGHT

The Nixon administration showed this ugly face of its working ideology—of the superimportance of government—even more clearly in its dealings with the *New York Times* in June 1971.

The Pentagon Papers demonstrated, among other things, that the Johnson administration was primarily responsible for guiding America into a major Asian land war through a consistent series of miscalculations of reality and deceptions of the American people. The time focus was 1963–65, so the exposé was largely historical—current history, perhaps, but history nonetheless. Six years is a reasonably long time: it is enough to age a fine bourbon, and a surfeit to change national administrations. In the six years since 1965, Lyndon B. Johnson had become a Texas library; Dean Rusk had proved that one can go home again; and McNamara was once again a ragtime band. Furthermore, since the cutoff date of the Pentagon study, the Nixon administration had publicly repudiated indefinite continuance in the Vietnam War and was, at the time of the public revelations, committed to "irreversible" military withdrawal.

As a matter of fact, the *Times*'s exposure of these papers could have worked to Nixon's resounding political benefit. Some Republican politicos were quick to react politically to the furor. Hugh Scott, the Republican Minority Leader in the U.S. Senate, observed that the documents damned Democrats and spotlighted intraparty squabbling. That was swift, sharp politics, a kind we foolishly trust characterizes our political system.

If the Nixon administration, as a group of top-echelon leaders, were truly interested in democratic politics (small *d*), it would have followed the Scott tack, or permitted the obvious implications of Democratic responsibility for the war through duplicity to become a *cause célèbre*. They might have added that the Pentagon Papers depicted the lengths to which Democrats would go to rob an election (1964).

But the Nixon administration did not see the Johnson or Kennedy administrations as party adversaries at all. They could see them only as former *government* officials, and their memos, letters, scribblings, and papers as *government* documents. That is what is so frightening about the intent to suppress what followed: not that it was the first time that an American government had moved to censor an American newspaper (which has been known to happen during wartime), but that it was so unpolitical, and so progovernment.

There can be no debate over the principle that a free press is indispensable to a free society and that the press has the responsibility to publish data that conflict with and contradict

35

governmental justifications of government policies. Governments, of course, have a need to withhold information from other governments. Some secrets may have to be kept from the aboriginal public as well, when they involve crucial matters of immediate and future political and military tactics and strategy. Obviously a press that would divulge such sensitive information along these lines, and would educate foreign governments or agents to future potentials and policies, would be irresponsible at best and treasonous at worst.

In the *Times*-Nixon case, however, what could be clearer than that the information involved had to do with *past* decisions, and held no clues to future military possibilities or policies? Could General Giap and the North Vietnamese High Command have been put in a better military position because of the papers? Did these disclosures tell our enemies anything they didn't know or couldn't guess at before? Not if they had been reading the *New York Times* carefully before—a few years before.

Some official defenders of the attempted censorship contended that the disclosures embarrassed friendly governments. That argument added weighty evidence to the contention that some officials would dishonor the truth before the American public before they would bring dishonor to a foreign government.

Other highly positioned defenders of the Nixon censorship of the *Times*, General Maxwell Taylor, for instance, claimed that censorship was justified on the basis that the disclosures weakened the internal security of the nation, since public confidence in the government was undermined. It seems hard to believe that any newspaper article could do that in this case; if anything weakened public confidence and faith in government, it was the governmental activity that the newspaper reported.

It is even more worrisome that so few people realized how devastating a blow the Nixon administration and the Burger Court dealt the First Amendment in the *New York Times* case. Only three justices of the Supreme Court categorically rejected the government's right to precensor the material by getting an injunction from lower courts. The majority of the Court reestablished itself as a supercensor, able and willing to judge whether the executive branch could demonstrate that the national security might be damaged by such disclosures.

That this system still allows the judiciary, a government agency, to decide such matters shows just how much government remains above and beyond the people's control. Can anyone with even an ounce of sense believe that Supreme Court justices have any special expertise to determine what published facts are, or are not, more or less detrimental to the national security? Their guess is as good, or as bad, as mine, and is probably worse than that of skilled journalists.

But having a free press means that the newsman's guess is not to be second-guessed by any government agent, including the Supreme Court. It is high time to admit that we have moved another step toward a semifree press, and that the *Times* case has allowed government to tighten its ranks against the freedom of the people to supervise their own government.

This sense of extra importance which characterizes so much of what government does, even within its authority, accounts for a good deal of the government anarchy described in the next five chapters.

3
Police
Anarchy

Man who fights law always loses;
same as grasshopper is always
wrong in argument with chicken.
                    —*Charlie Chan*

Hi Mom! was a motion picture that circulated around some New York City art movie theaters during the spring and summer of 1970. It was black humor with red pepper, and it received mixed to good reviews. Perhaps the most effective and most memorable scene was the film's reproduction of a guerrilla theater play called *Be Black, Baby.*

Guerrilla theater is an attempt by performers to encircle and capture (though not necessarily captivate) an audience for political ends. It is a marriage of confrontation theater and confrontation politics. One type of this contemporary theater is the put-on; that is, the actors try to persuade the audience to act out roles as well—even though the audience is uncertain anyone is acting at all. In other words, the performers try to blur the theatricality of the event, thereby inducing direct involvement. Hopefully, when it is over the audience comes to realize the political point the guerrilla company wished to make, because the audience felt (rather than understood) that point. According to guerrilla theater people, only by being "had" can an audience have a political experience, and only by this method can a new level of political awareness be traded by the actors to the audience.

In *Be Black, Baby,* the actors, all but two of whom were black, wished to show the all-white audience how it felt to be black. "Understanding" liberal rhetoric on the black plight was not enough; the guerrilla company wanted whites to suffer the indignities and humiliation of being a "nigger."

First the audience was put into blackface. The (apparently) all-black cast had on whiteface. After having some "soul food" forced on them, the new-black audience was herded upstairs into a hallway, all the while being harassed by the actors with taunts, thinly veiled threats, and confusing statements. The actors kept the audience off balance by reminding them it was all a play. This was not overly reassuring to the members of the audience; how could they be certain it was a play?

Finally an actor, one of the white members of the cast planted among the audience, pulled a gun and told the black actors their game was over. He wanted out. The other members of the audience, relieved, went over to his side and followed him into a back elevator. Once the escaping audience reached the bottom floor, they found themselves surrounded by angry "whites," other actors. The new-blacks had been betrayed by an infiltrator. The "whites" began to terrorize the "blacks." One of them actually raped one of the "black" women in the elevator.

At last a "policeman" came on the scene, but he was the other white actor in the troupe. His role was to react favorably to the "whites" and to systematically abuse the "blacks." Remember that one of the "blacks" had just been raped. This was reported to him by one of the new-niggers (who didn't know the real white cop was another actor) and the cop's first response was to line all the "blacks" against the wall and search them. Then he asked each of them for identification, since it was a black-white melee, with reported violence, and we all know that when violence is reported among whites and blacks, the likelihood is greater that the blacks started it.

This, of course, enraged the new-niggers, since one of their women had been raped. Some protested. This kind of situation could also lead to insulting an officer, who naturally would resent the implication (if not explication) of prejudice. He would react by pushing the one who complained, which in turn would be met with some resistance, and thence an arrest on a variety of charges from disturbing the peace through resisting arrest to impeding the administration of justice.

But the fact was that the policeman created the situation that led to the arrest, by the natural and understandable conditioned response of his professional mind. It was his fault that there was any shoving and pushing. He was derelict in his duty in not apprehending the only and real felon, the "white" rapist. Such police actions, done routinely, are acts of anarchy. In being biased and partial, they are beyond the law and lead to further violence. Such actions by many policemen, even without any philosophy of anarchy, are islands of anarchy, erupting in time and space, in black oceans, throughout America. They make up the daily fare of ordinary abuse heaped upon any disfavored group throughout American society.

Another guerrilla theater presentation along these lines, billed as a "very multi-media political experiment . . . inspired by the 50th Anniversary Celebration of the American Civil Liberties Union," occurred at the Electric Circus, in New York City, on June 4, 1970. The audience was comprised of approximately 250 delegates to the biennial conference of the ACLU. The "stage" was the whole building in which the Electric Circus was housed, although the audience was unaware of this as it entered.

Upon reaching a table at the front door, each member of the audience was told that stringent security measures were in effect because of a bomb threat. Everyone was asked to identify himself before being admitted to the theater. There were several lists of names, and each person was (arbitrarily) assigned a color (red, green, and blue). Those who were designated green were cordially welcomed. "Reds" were politely detained for further "preliminary investigation." "Blues" were hustled upstairs blindfolded, past the main showroom, and underwent a sharp and embarrassing interrogation. In this theatrical experience, no physical force was used at any point; people were detained or searched only if they voluntarily submitted to verbal authority.

The "interrogators" were played by a New York City acting company known as the Performance Group.[1] The performers assumed several roles that police play, from good-guy interrogator to a more sadistic type. They aimed to make people experience some of the humiliation inherent in all types of inter-

43

rogation, particularly when the "suspect" is innocent, and even more particularly where security measures are obvious overreactions to any observable threat.

Meanwhile, in the main hall on the second floor, another acting company, the Theatre of Encounter,[2] had divided itself into several components, each with distinctive roles. One, the "Electric Circus Internal Security Force," was introduced by an actor posing as a Circus official. The "greens," who were the remnants of the audience, were informed that these security officers were instructed to enforce a few reasonable rules: (1) no smoking; (2) no leaning against the walls; (3) no stepping on several tape squares that covered (fake) electronic connections (the audience was warned that if these squares were scuffed or stomped, the show would probably be disrupted); and (4) no drugs. The audience was also told the security force had electronic detectors that would register all metal (even an excess of coins in a purse) since they had to guard against the possibility of a concealed bomb.

Throughout the course of the multi-media show entitled *Government Anarchy?* the internal security force committed an increasing set of illegal acts, all of which some police are accused of perpetrating on their daily rounds. For instance, there were the annoying superfluous identity checks (there had already been a check at the door), repeated searches for bombs (there was little reason to fear them), and continual negligent encroachment on the right of patrons to enjoy the show (for instance, flashing lights into the faces of some people while searching others).

Both productions were motivated by the deep conviction that police lawlessness had better be mildly felt, as well as strongly understood intellectually. Many daily victims of official anarchy wish their sympathizers could feel what it is like to be hit, hounded, hit, harassed, hit, hunted, hit, hindered, and hassled by police. They know that feeling can move them as no thought can. It hurts even more when the victim is innocent, or singled out for special treatment on the basis of "reasonable or probable suspicion" (those with long hair are often suspected of carrying marijuana or "being under the influence") or on the basis of his politics. But in this book we will have to settle for more conventional, linear means to describe some of the many types of police lawlessness that are coming to light these days.

For instance, a growing number of reports described excessive harassment by New Jersey State Police on the New Jersey Turnpike. Apparently some state troopers considered it their duty (or good sport) to stop and thoroughly comb cars driven by young men who eschewed the crewcut. The whole process was time-consuming and costly in terms of individual dignity. But aside from the fact that the ACLU brought suit for an injunction on behalf of thirty-seven complainants, there is little that can be done currently to retard this practice.

A rather simple experiment conducted by a professor at California State College, Los Angeles,[3] suggests that New Jersey police are not alone in their understanding of what is legal on the highway. He decided to test a complaint by black students that they were discriminated against by the Highway Patrol, particularly if they pasted Black Panther bumper stickers on their cars. He recruited fifteen students (equally divided between blacks, whites, and chicanos), making sure that each had a flawless driving record for a whole year past. Each was educated on the rules for driving in California, and each swore to continue driving safely within the law. Each was given a black and orange Black Panther sticker to attach to his car, and set off on his own. Remember that none of these drivers had received a summons for a moving violation for at least a year.

"The first student received a ticket for making an 'incorrect lane change' on the freeway less than two hours after heading home." Five more summonses were issued the next day to the experimental group (for following too closely, driving too slow, and incorrect signaling). The third day, three more tickets were received.

One student was forced to drop out of the study by day four, because he had already received three citations. Three others reached what we had agreed was the maximum limit—three citations—within the first week. Altogether, the participants received 33 citations in 17 days. . . .

On the brighter side, darker students fared no worse than lighter ones.

An article in *Trans/Action*, entitled "How Common Is Police Brutality?" quotes a New York City police commissioner:

For three years, there has been through the courts and streets a dreary procession of citizens with broken heads and bruised bodies against few of whom was violence needed to effect an arrest. Many of them had done nothing to deserve an arrest. In a majority of such cases, no complaint was made. If the victim complains, his charge is generally dismissed. The police are practically above law.[4]

What is most engaging about the quote is that it was originally published in *1903!* The author of the article, Albert Reiss, Jr., a prominent sociologist, believes that police brutality is still "far from rare." In addition to mashed heads, he feels that unnecessary shoving and pushing and prodding people with clubs are part of the definition of "police brutality." He feels, moreover, that threats of force and abusive language from an armed man might also be brutish, if not brutal.

Reiss conducted a study of police brutality in Boston, Chicago, and Washington, D.C., during the summer of 1966, where he engaged thirty-six researchers from the Center for Research on Social Organization to make the rounds with policemen and observe their behavior. His findings give us a rough indicator of the extent of actual brutality.

For example, of 643 white suspects, 27 of them were subjected to undue use of force. This yields an abuse rate of 41.9 per 1000, or 4.19 percent. The comparable rate for 751 Negro suspects was 22.6 per 1000, or 2.26 per cent. The combined rate for some 1400 people was slightly over 3 percent, and these acts of police brutality were committed *while outside observers were watching them.*

What's 3 percent? Each year in America, there are over 4.5 million arrests. These particular incidents took place under scrutiny, and this study was conducted in three of our largest and most enlightened cities. Of the 4.5 million yearly American arrestees, approximately one quarter of them were released after arrest with no charges brought against them.[5] In other words, after arrest, police officials themselves felt there was insufficient evidence to hold the suspects. More often than not, the arrests were probably due to either poor police work, incompetence, or malice. That means that some 1 million Americans each year are arrested for no good reason. Applying the very conservative 3 percent figure to them, that would mean that 30,000 Americans are physically abused each year by the police for no good reason. Even if charge were made to stick after arrest, that would still not justify police abusiveness. And this percentage doesn't count police brutality that does not precede arrest.

Very little is done to remedy the situation, that is, to treat unjustified physical brutality and unjustified arrest by police as harshly as we would treat brutality on police. For instance, from 1940 to 1968, all of four reports were published of criminal prosecutions against police officers for their misconduct, and all were for false imprisonment. Four in twenty-nine years.[6] Even with the indictment of six Los Angeles policemen for various crimes—manslaughter, assault, conspiracy to burglarize, and deprivation of civil rights—by a federal grand jury in March 1971, the indictment gap remains wide and shows no trend toward closing too drastically.

Many intellectuals, pseudo-intellectuals, anti-intellectuals, liberals, conservatives, and moderates know about this, but few have come face to face with the billy-club end of the problem themselves.

The guerrilla theater productions described above try to drill the point home—to the gut level, the origin of all important

47

political reforms. Being theater, however, these productions could not begin to display the entire garland of weeds that ordinary police lawlessness is and can be. The whole truth is much worse.

POLICE RIOTS

The highly publicized urban riots of the sixties and the debacle in Chicago in 1968 pushed some islands of police anarchy into the naked view of some important sewing circles in America. This has been particularly true of mob actions by throngs of police. In the cities, outbreaks of large-scale police violence have been experienced and feared by black communities for some time. Police riots did not originate in Chicago, but the 1968 Chicago police riot was a revelation to many whites unfortunate enough to stray near the scene of the demonstrations. And it typified the worst of a genre that extends from maxibrawls to riots—police stoked and stimulated.

The police riot, distinguishable from other crowd-control activities, is characterized by an avalanche of uniformed police, usually preceded by a yellow cloud of gas, enveloping a retreating mass of people. A general crunching and crashing of clubs and fists on the head, shoulders, arms, buttocks, and legs of anyone—newsmen, photographers, and cameramen are particularly appealing objects—is also usually part of the scene.

During the center-staging of the riot act, one can also watch police-directed side shows: stomping people who are down, aggravating injuries upon people already injured, and ganging up on small groups of people some police are particularly eager to get. The finale is not as easily appreciated, since it is usually performed off-stage. Small groups of police dart from the main ring and whale the daylights out of small pockets of the enemy in back alleys, police cars, police vans, or even—in rare cases—private retreats.

One performance in Boston bears repeating since it was less ballyhooed than some others—for a number of reasons: (1) there was not much property damage, (2) no one was killed, and (3) there were no obviously national political overtones. It was just a good old spontaneous local police riot against some average students and "street people." Also, since it was short-lived and involved only several hundred people, it might best be called a police miniriot.

There is a Back Bay section of Boston populated largely by a hodgepodge of students, artists, dropouts, and quasi-degenerates. Many of them attended, taught at, or were affiliated in some way with Northeastern University.

During the stress surrounding the Cambodian adventure and the gunning down of students at Kent State and Jackson State, a series of late-evening "block parties" were thrown by the denizens of Hemenway Street, a main drag in this section. Because of the student strikes and warmer springtime weather, students were not inclined to sleep early. Around eleven each evening, students congregated in the streets, strumming guitars, singing, drinking, skimming frisbees, and of course, smoking the devil weed. The get-togethers lasted until three or four each morning. In the natural order of things, complaints began to accumulate in the adjacent precincts, and the Boston police were compelled to deal with the nuisance.

To the everlasting credit of the police, it was said that they were highly cooperative for the first few nights. Although some minor skirmishes were reported after their first major attempt to stop these evening events, nothing terribly serious developed until the Sunday "party." In defense of the police, it should be noted that: (1) several laws were being violated, and some people in the neighborhood demanded the enforcement of their right to sleep; (2) student radicals, determined to resist the police, had made their intentions known; and (3) extreme verbal and some physical provocations were the order of the night. And

49

as has come to happen, some police totally lost their cool. For instance:

Item:

> . . . a blind student at Berkley School of Music, sitting on the steps with his wife, recalls, "I heard people shouting 'Here they come,' so I turned and walked up the steps to our first floor apartment. I had my key out and was trying to fit it into the lock when I heard this tremendous smash of glass and then these blows hitting my head." His wife, who was following closely behind her husband, says that six to eight policemen broke through a glass door and began clubbing both of them. "We kept yelling 'We live here' but they just kept flailing away. Then they just turned around and ran out."

The reporter of this event noted that both victims received multiple stitches in their heads at a local hospital.

Item:

> Meanwhile, several students recall, a group of policemen had reached [a] roof. . . . A resident assistant . . . says he saw 10 policemen standing on the roof "throwing pipes, rocks, stones and anything else they could find onto the sidewalk, parked cars, and people." Four Northeastern freshmen in the same dormitory . . . report seeing the same thing. . . . "It was incredible. I saw this policeman hold a huge rock over the edge of the roof and then drop it directly on the roof of this green Plymouth." [7]

The article describes other similar incidents. It also reports that some policemen were heard cheering, "Kent State got four. We want more."

Actually, to one who has labored over stacks of government staff reports, newspaper articles, and civil liberties union reports, the Boston miniriot, though classic, does suffer from a lack of extraordinary atrocities. There are no reports of motorcycle police trying to run citizens down (discussed in the Walker report on the Chicago event), no pot-shooting at imagined "snipers," no reports of police yanking people from vehicles (New York Moratorium incident), no camera smashings, and no regimental pincer movements. That's why this incident must be put in its place. It doesn't quite reach the velocity and ferocity of the full-blown riots, e.g., Chicago; People's Park; Isla Vista; Watts. It is, no more, no less, a miniriot.

When I went to observe the November 1969 Moratorium march in Washington D.C., I did my best to steer clear of announced trouble spots. On Saturday night, however, three friends and I went to a restaurant in the vicinity of Dupont Circle. About 10:30 P.M., we decided to window-shop in the Circle area, but heard a commotion a block or so away.

We went to find out what was happening, but a few teen-age scouts warned us the police were on their way. Their grapevine was accurate enough. From nowhere, a skirmish line of police appeared behind us—a solid, moving wall. We wondered why they were there, for although something was burning in the middle of the Circle, there was no uncontrollable crowd, no observable threat. It was a manageable bonfire with a few people milling around. That was all. But the police began what one told me was a "sweep" of the area.

We watched them pounce on several youngsters who were in their way and club them severely. They had done nothing. Two police ordered me to "get out of here." At that moment a canister of tear gas fell about ten feet from me, cutting off my own retreat as well as that of a dozen other people. Fortunately the wind carried the fumes in the opposite direction.

This affair was neither a police "riot" nor even a "miniriot." It was a police "maxibrawl," an outstanding example of the way in which some of these rather lopsided contests do not escalate because the citizens can and do decide to forgo resistance to an obvious police overreaction.

These police tactics, often justified as "an ounce of prevention," are illegal in and of themselves when innocent people happen to be around, as they inevitably are. Does it make any difference to the public at large whether a band of men, bent on mugging anyone in their path, wears blue uniforms? It is hard to believe that the police themselves would deny they could do the job less expensively, more surgically, and avoid injuring innocent people. But they will risk a maximum amount of damage to innocents in order to minimize injury to themselves.

In their view, it is necessary to flood an area with police and clear it completely in order to protect themselves. To be sure, they say they want to prevent an escalation of the incident that would cause even more personal injury to more innocent people. But that is the same outworn logic generals use to justify preemptive war. It violates that part of our legal code reserving punishment for people who have committed a crime and arrest for specific, identified individuals under reasonable suspicion for specific crimes.

Such maraudings are official anarchy. The police are paid to take risks to their physical well-being—and not to minimize that risk at the expense of a helpless citizenry. Yet even when maxibrawls and miniriots are clearly police-instigated in part, and innocent people are injured or killed, weak or no sanctions follow. For instance, in 1971 *Newsweek* did a follow-up story on the 1969 Jackson State police riot. The reporter noted that "despite investigations by two grand juries and the Scranton Commission on Campus Unrest—and astonishing revelations of bloodthirstiness, ineptitude and outright lies on the part of the police—not a single person involved in the killings has been punished. What's more, apparently no one will be.[8]

POLICE INFILTRAITORS

There is yet another type of police riot in which police do not participate, at least not officially.

A few days after the Kent State incident, about a thousand students, most of them from NYU, announced a massive intrusion into the Wall Street section of New York City to advertise their displeasure with the Cambodia incursion and to try to induce similar Wall Street sentiment to surface. What arose was something decidedly less desirable.

The students arrived downtown and began to do what it was they came to do. They launched antiwar missiles. They discussed Cambodia and Kent with anyone who wore ears. They congregated in a large group and listened to speakers. Then the lunch break arrived and the peace broke.

A battalion of construction workers, hardhatted and hardboiled, converged on the peace group and began to pummel them and anyone who seemed unfriendly to such hardheaded tactics. The more than two hundred construction workers regrouped after their initial sortie, and churned in another direction —toward the most readily available enemy fortress, the brandnew student union at Pace College. Some of their number charged into the building and did a deconstruction job on it, as well as on some of the students too amazed to run for cover.

This was a quasi-police riot because of the inaction of the police who were around. Strangely enough, with all that broaddaylight battering going on, there were only six reported arrests, remarkable considering the fact that approximately fifty people were injured.[9] One need not stretch one's imagination to think how many people would have become candidates for the Black Maria had the Weathermen and Weatherwomen gone around beating on pedestrians in Chicago or anywhere.

To anyone watching parts of this slaughter on television that evening, it was a revealing scene, to say the least. Lines of policemen, arms extended, were holding helmeted construction workers back from the peace rally. Then one could see some hardnoses going under the outstretched arms of some police. Soon, some blue arms went down, and more destruction workers filtered through. A few close-ups showed policemen feebly holding the arms of workers and smiling once they slipped their butter grip.

It seemed clear that the police were by and large in sympathy with the message and methods of the workers. The fact that the workers' tactics were illicit and violent failed to move most of the police on duty. And incidents similar to this one, involving demonstrations by construction workers in Chicago, and anti-construction workers in Pittsburgh late in 1969, saw massive police inaction in response to violence and lawbreaking on the one hand and substantial response to it on the other. The critical variable is who is marching: [10] Strangely, when violence erupts in a construction worker march there are very few arrests. However, in Pittsburgh, when "hundreds" of blacks and white sympathizers marched against racial discrimination in the construction industry, 122 were jailed for the "scuffling" that ensued.[11]

Miniriots can sometimes be supported by police through complicity, though not by active police participation. This is not to say that there is any prior plotting between the police and their *avant-garde*. There does not have to be. A spontaneous riot with police help can be worse than a planned one.

The fact that police have been known to use unofficial and unrehearsed agents to occasion a riot or maxibrawl has raised another hackle or two of late. Undercover agents, working for government agencies, do not simply infiltrate enemy lines: they become the enemy. What is even worse, they sometimes become enemy leaders.

For instance, sometime in 1969, a young, dark-haired man arrived at Hobart College in New York. "Tommy the Traveler's" claim to fame was that he was a hot-shot organizer for SDS, a missionary of revolution and a teacher of violent methods, including serving Molotov cocktails at revolutionary parties. In addition to his proselytizing and fiery delivery, Tommy managed to display a hot temper. On one occasion, he punched the assistant dean of students (assault and battery) and another time threatened the life of a "fellow student." According to *Time* magazine,[12] Tommy left a wake of disturbances behind him. At Cornell, Syracuse, or Alfred—wherever he showed up—"violence seemed to follow."

According to *Time*, in order to produce some arrests on the Hobart campus, Tommy had to blow his cover. By doing this, however, he raised the dander of many people around Hobart, and an investigation ensued. Apparently this fellow Traveler worked for a government agency and did this sort of thing professionally. The local sheriff didn't think much was wrong with the practice. According to him and most police officials, such undercover actions were essential to establish the credibility of infiltrators.

There can be little doubt that secret police agents are officially privileged to break laws while undercover, but there *is* doubt whether it is necessary, and whether such latitude should be given to a government official in a democratic society. Certainly there is no statutory license for such crimes. Police officials have rewritten the law to serve their goals.

Another specific instance: the case of "Prince George Crazy" Demmerle, arrested with three comrades in the fall of 1969 in New York City, on bombing charges. This group, responsible for a rash of bombings of several New York buildings, was caught red-handed attempting to transform several National Guard trucks into twisted wreckage. Shortly after their booking, it became known that Demmerle was released—scot-free—and word spread that he was a police agent, undercover for some time.

Prince George Crazy did not acquire his name from the New York City Police Department; he earned it from his fans, among the weirdest weirdos in all America. He was, in a word, outstanding, in a very fast league. According to some sources, no one ever saw him "off a trip." Demmerle would sit at Yippie meetings playing with toy bombs he had fabricated. Among his other ventures, he was one of the leaders of a group of "Crazies" that forcefully disrupted a Nagasaki Day rally sponsored by the Fifth Avenue Peace Parade Committee.

The cloak-and-dagger tales that made such good movies in the forties and the fifties, wherein cool, patriotic men risked their lives to enlist in organizations devoted to destroying America were good war stories. Starched Nazis, seedy Russians, and sneaky Japs—all were fair targets for undercover work. But then, that was a war brought upon the United States of America, one in which national survival was at stake. The situation is far different today. The analogy that government wishes to make is not terribly convincing. Although police agencies like to claim that the situation is similar, it is in their own personal and organizational self-interest to make such arguments.

American radicals have every right short of violent action to subvert our form of government, whereas foreigners have no such right at all. In any event, no legislative and certainly no constitutional license exists as yet for government agents to break laws systematically and to teach and lead other Americans into a criminal, if not treasonous, life. If it was true that Boyd Douglas, the FBI informer in the Harrisburg Seven case, actually recruited several of his coed girlfriends for the alleged conspiracy, is this what Government agents should be paid to do? Should they be privileged to become kingpins in the crime— essential to the planning and the attempts—and then be immune from prosecution? How far does this go? Too far, when leaders of the 1970 San Jose anti-Nixon demonstration felt called upon to tell a rally the evening before that "anyone who throws rocks will be considered a police provocateur." [13]

POLICE CONSPIRACIES

The word "conspiracy" has received a lot of publicity recently. The main reason has been congressional lust to tag, gag, and bag highly vocal and militant groups in this country, particularly those that rate a national image. Whether they are well organized, poorly organized, or disorganized is not important. Congressmen want as many legal hooks as possible to hinder or neutralize the most garrulous and influential individuals in "the movement."

New conspiracy laws have been devised and, whenever possible, dormant ones revived. Their perennial popularity stems from the fact that the charge of conspiracy is sometimes the only (and frequently the most efficient) way to paralyze a political enemy since acts are not a necessary part of the crime. In point of fact, mere words can constitute conspiracy. So, although leaders may be canny enough to avoid doing, they cannot avoid talking and still be leaders.

The traditional common-law crime of conspiracy usually connoted a small, closely knit group of people collaborating to commit an illegality. This necessitated meetings, planning, review of tactics, and preliminary actions, though it did not require dark rooms, candle-topped bottles, and other sinister accoutrements. The contemporary concept of conspiracy needs none of this. All that matters these days, whether it be conspiracy to impede the draft or conspiracy to cross state lines with the intent to incite a riot, is that the parties involved make *open* statements indicating their own personal *approval* of illegal acts that *might* be committed *by their audience (or anyone)*. These statements must be made with knowledge that the coconspirators were (probably) making similar statements. Although it helps the prosecution if all the alleged coconspirators said their piece in each other's immediate presence, even that is not a *sine qua non* of the new government concept of conspiracy.

This more flexible notion of conspiracy, interestingly enough, supports the allegation that police commit conspiracies too. The most highly publicized charge of "police conspiracy" (in this expanded sense) has been made by the Black Panther Party. Over the past few years, the BPP has suffered grievous casualties from actions by local police departments across the country. The list includes dead, wounded, and missing in action (those in jail pending trial with bail too high for them to pay).

According to the American Civil Liberties Union, from 1967 to 1969 in sixteen cities, 12 Panthers were killed by police and 12 were wounded, while 3 police died and some 24 were wounded. Another source, Charles R. Garry, chief counsel of the national BPP, claimed that 28 Panthers actually had been killed during this same period of time. Garry was closely questioned on this by the *New York Times* and he quickly reduced the grand total to 19 who "died violently." Of the nineteen, 7 were killed other than in direct confrontation with police forces. So, as the *San Francisco Examiner* observed, the 28 shrank to 12, "by Mr. Garry's own telling." The *Examiner* also noted that one of the 12 was Alex Rackley, who was probably the victim of the Panthers themselves, as a New Haven jury determined. "Only" 11 were killed in shoot-outs with the police, including the famous homicide of Panthers Clark and Fred Hampton in Chicago in 1969.

Whatever the exact figure, a death toll this size hardly amounts to "genocide," as the new left has charged. On the other hand, the precise size of the obituary is of no greater value in understanding the social, economic, and political aspects of the problem than is the body count in Vietnam.

The fact is that some police and Black Panthers like each other not one whit. Black Panthers and their associates have published menus of roasted pig, crisp bacon, and pork chops, contrasting sharply with the peace orientation of their breakfast plan. But the Panthers' menacing posture, even couched in terms of self-defense, plus their bristling arsenals, posed mortal danger to many police with no particular grudge against black people. In other words, many cops are understandably jumpy about being gunned down by lunatic-fringe militants.* Some other police who bitterly hate blacks in general turn livid at the sight of blacks wearing bandoliers and cradling shotguns in their arms.

Considering the historical, sociological, psychological, and economic antagonisms involved, incidents like the Chicago police

---

* For instance, two policemen were killed by sniper fire in Chicago in June 1970. They were on "walk and talk" patrols—a police program to help alleviate tensions between the police and the black community, and both were known to be friendly to the black community. And the 1971–72 season shows some signs of a loose national federation of black gunmen who see themselves as avengers, free to murder any policeman, white or black.

commando raid into a Black Panther lair and several other show-downs have been surprising only for their infrequency. On the other hand, the Panthers are, at least in part, a black response to general societal and specific police abuse of the black com-munity—and of specific abuses by individual policemen on specific black people. The party has a legitimate beef, a right to organize, and a right to defend itself against unlawful violence.

Clearly the problem of mortal enmity by some police toward the Black Panther Party, some currently more militant splinter groups, or against blacks in general is a national one. Some po-lice, across the country, talk about "getting" Panthers, and some of the incidents probably stem directly from this attitude as well as general antiblack feelings. The affliction, by the way, is not limited to the cop on the beat. For instance, William Turner, a former FBI agent, noted that "during my career in law enforce-ment, I found that there exists a broad band of animosity toward political and racial minorities. In the FBI, for example, agents often referred to an automobile occupied by Negroes as 'a load of coal,' and scurrilous remarks of this nature are common in private talk among officers." [14]

Many other incidents are probably caused by overly bitter blacks and still others by mutual and reciprocally hostile ac-tions. But the number of police-inspired or -instigated incidents would represent the incidence and breadth of the "police con-spiracy" against militant black organizations, just as new left rhetoric is "conspiratorial," as it results in coincidental or con-current, though unorganized, national terrorism.

A police conspiracy probably exists to some degree and should be squashed as quickly as any similar conspiracy to vio-late laws among citizens outside of government. Each police-black organization shooting match should be investigated hon-estly, and in great depth. All policemen involved should be subjected to a thorough investigation into their attitudes toward various black organizations, their statements about Panthers and blacks in general, and their actions in the black community, in order to determine the possibility of premeditation. In fact, investigation should be made of all police suspected of malice toward black people to see if they had made inflammatory remarks that could have incited other policemen to act lawlessly. If words are to be criminal behavior, the police must be as accountable as other Americans.

But police hostility toward cliques is not limited to Black Panthers, their friends, imitators, and offspring. Many studies indicate that policemen are recruited heavily from economic and social classes often characterized by a certain narrowness of viewpoint on living styles and firmly held prejudices against outgroups. Many policemen find the contemporary life-style of the so-called counterculture, made up primarily of the progeny of the upper and upper middle classes, peculiarly distasteful. For one thing, the low esteem in which dirt and sexual promiscuity are held, as well as the traditional sanctity of cleanliness, neatness, comfort, position, sophistication, and higher education among working-class people, often brings them into conflict with a counterculture which of course repudiates all this in ideal and practice. When counterculture individuals act out their rejection, they rankle the working class, and consequently many policemen. This has been called "the residual hostility of the police" by the Task Force on Law Enforcement for Milton Eisenhower's Commission on the Causes and Prevention of Violence.[15] So some police undoubtedly consider it their sworn duty to crack the heads of these people, and they take pains to find them. The result could be considered a coast-to-coast "police conspiracy" to eliminate these evils; many policemen talk about remedying the situation, and it is a nationwide phenomenon.

There are many opportunities for individual policemen (as well as groups of them) to harass and disperse gatherings of "hippies" as unceremoniously as possible, whenever it is politically feasible. In these actions, the police trample on any number of laws themselves. They physically and verbally abuse, they exhibit far more brawn than necessary, they book people indiscriminately, and they lie about what those under arrest have done. They are also frequently accused of planting contraband, like marijuana, in order to provide a reason to act.

Two now legendary police sweeps against elements of the counterculture were the Tompkins Square Park massacre in the East Village of New York on May 30, 1967, and a Los Angeles Police Department blitzkrieg of a Venice Beach be-in, also in 1967. Abbie Hoffman saw a "certain police pattern" materializing and the *East Village Other* referred to these incidents as a developing "national coincidence." But it can also be called conspiracy, as currently redefined.

If America no longer needs a cabal of conspirators or even agreement among independent malefactors, but simply requires parallel crimes here and there—preceded by talk about "what needs to be done"—then we may have a rather large-scale police conspiratorial network in operation. There need be no surreptitious nationwide police Cosa Nostra, mutually scheming to obliterate hippies, Panthers, or some other particularly police-obnoxious group. There simply needs to be a pattern or coincidence of action along these lines, precipitated by unconnected but similar talking about the need and desirability for it to be done.

For those who might be appalled at calling *government* acts conspiracy, there is expert opinion to substantiate the fact that the first conspiracy statutes in English law were directed against government itself. Conspiracy, from the beginning, was a crime among officials to deprive individuals of their personal rights. One could only bring a conspiracy charge, though, upon being absolved of a criminal charge in a court of law; then one could sue the officers for conspiring to do him in. So a charge of conspiracy among government officials is in the best of tradition. It is no radical idea at all.

CONTEMPT OF COURT

As far as I know, no one has ever been accused or cited for contempt of court for anything said or done before the United States Supreme Court. In fact, almost every contempt charge is for some statement or action "in the face" of a trial court. That is to say that a party, or a lawyer, or someone who is a part of the audience, acts in some way or says something to the judge that the judge considers unpardonable. This happens more than often enough since many judges seem to invest a lot of personal ego in the "dignity of the court."

But there is another kind of contempt of court. This involves a person, subject to a judgment, who refuses to comply with the mandate of the court. If he persists in his defiance, the court has the power to judge him in contempt and to jail him until obeisance is forthcoming. For example, if a husband withholds alimony, the judge may commit him to jail until he promises to maintain his wife's legally ordained security.

To the best of my knowledge, though, no one has ever been cited and jailed for contempt of court for refusing to comply with a mandate of the United States Supreme Court. There are several reasons for this. One of them is that the ultimate disposition of the case is frequently the responsibility of a state court, and the individual involved will be directed by that lower court to do or not do something. Thus any contempt is of that lower court. For another, the Supreme Court makes *general* policies that tell large groups of people (e.g., Seventh-Day Adventists, police, demonstrators) what they can or cannot do. Thus the behavior of such groups becomes a question of law enforcement, not court enforcement—at least at first.

But this last point seems to make a meaningless distinction. For if the Supreme Court directs *all* teachers to stop reading prayers in public schools, then that is, in a real sense, a direction of that court to each and every one of them, personally, as they play the role of teacher. If any of them insist on disobeying and persist in doing so, it seems to me to be contempt of (Supreme) court.

If this is a government of law and not of men, and if the Constitution is the supreme law of the land, and if the Supreme Court is the supreme interpreter of that law, then a clear direction from the Court as to what must be done must be obeyed. When it is not, it is contempt of court. And it is equally true whether the public official be a school teacher, or a governor, or a policeman. I'd like to mention the mounting evidence that describes the extent of some police contempt of the Supreme Court.

Many if not most police officials carp about the naïveté of the Supreme Court (particularly "The Warren Court") regarding police behavior toward suspects, detainees, and arrestees. They are fond of saying things like the Court has "shackled" or "hand-cuffed" the police and thus hampered their perilous but relentless pursuit of felons. To their way of thinking, the Court has placed priority on the "rights of criminals" instead of on the "rights of citizens" to be protected against criminals.

Many American political scientists, historians, and statesmen have properly observed from time to time that there is a painful conflict built into the Constitution between the rights of citizens and the duties of government. The police, naturally, want to catch criminals; that is what they are in business for. The police will always find it more difficult to fight crime with the restrictions placed on them in the American Bill of Rights—which is just as much the law of the land as any statute prohibiting the possession of narcotics. It is perfectly understandable that many policemen fail to see that it is certainly of equal (if not greater) priority to shield innocent people against unjust persecution as it is to make the apprehension of criminals as easy as possible.

Others believe that a semi-police state is worse than a state of semianarchy. So the struggle for both positions is transformed into a political one. Police brassdom is itself a formidable political force, constantly seeking legislation to extend police prerogatives, personnel, and power. And this is fine. It is well within the rules of the democratic game. The police arguments must be heard, and they deserve fair response.

But police defy that component of government that makes the final decision on these matters, that is, the Supreme Court and its local affiliates. In America, the official expertise on things constitutional rests with the nine men and their subordinates. When they speak, that is the law—unless and until something is done within the political process to change their mandate. And the Court has spoken clearly, directly, and with vigor in recent years on how the police must act toward people under suspicion of committing crimes. No one is a criminal until he either confesses to it or is convicted in a court of law. It is not the rights of criminals that the police care to have curbed; it is the rights of citizens.

Many policemen have been and are too impatient to wait for the political process to reverse what the courts insist upon. They simply call plays to be run out of bounds; they decide to act in contempt of the Supreme Court and of the local courts. And the extent to which this occurs is a large vein of official anarchy still coursing throughout the body politic.

The decisions of *Escobedo v. Illinois* (1964) [16] and *Miranda v. Arizona* (1966) [17] were denounced by many police officials and politicians in favor of more strict law enforcement. Each of these cases required the police to follow stringent guidelines in informing people under arrest of their rights. Among the guidelines: (1) anything the suspect says can be used against him, (2) he has an absolute right to remain silent, (3) he has a right to counsel, and (4) he has a right to have counsel present *at the interrogation*. Obviously, providing this information would make it more difficult for the police to extract confessions from people. But it was and is the law.

A group of law students from Yale University received permission from local authorities to conduct a summer-long study of how the New Haven police reacted in practice to this new law. They were allowed to plant themselves at the police station, even in the previously sacrosanct interrogation rooms, in order to observe whether police behavior conformed with the new Supreme Court guidelines. And so they did, shift after shift of them, watching the police grilling suspect after suspect. It was a unique experiment in cooperation between a local constabulary and a local law school.

Their findings came out a year or so later, and among the more positive revelations was the fact that during that summer, there was a notable increase in Miranda-type warnings given to suspects. Happily, "only 22 percent of the suspects were not advised at all of their constitutional rights." [18] (*Only?*) And, happily, there was a substantial increase in the percentage of full and partial Miranda warnings given to suspects during the summer.

What is more important is that many police officers, fully cognizant of what they were doing, systematically broke the law, both in its letter and its spirit, in the performance of their duties. For instance, look at these findings by the Yale group: "Despite the presence of our observers in the police station, the detectives gave all the advice required by Miranda to only 25 of 118 suspects questioned." That approximates an 80 percent police contempt of court! And that with outside witnesses observing them!

Even when detectives followed the formal requirements of Miranda, they managed to water them down with ingenuity and aplomb—enough so that suspects could be unsure of their rights, which is what the Supreme Court had tried to prevent. For instance, some would say that whatever the suspect said could be used "*for* or against him" in court. Others would tell the suspect, after informing him of his right to remain silent, that he had better speak up. Furthermore, about 15 percent of the suspects underwent "coercive interrogations." What is most interesting about these is that they were no more successful in prying confessions and admissions out of the suspects than noncoercive ones.

However, not all police contempt is beyond judicial eyeshot. A good deal of it occurs right under the judge's spectacles. This is the problem of police cover charges and police perjury. In fact, Paul Chevigny, an eminent civil liberties attorney, calls the extent of police lying while under oath the "gravest abuse" that police commit.[19] That's debatable, of course, but the extent of this practice is known by attorneys to be vast.

It is not that policemen are inveterate liars, have some unique quarrel with truth, or are particularly malicious. But a healthier than average amount of self-righteousness and identification of self with "the law" by many police leads to much conscience-free rupturing of the truth.

As Chevigny points out, the policeman who finds his authority challenged on the beat takes it personally. And even though a local yokel may be breaking no law, his challenge indicates a disrespect for the law in general and constitutes a more probable threat to law and order in the eyes of the policeman. The arrest that may follow is for "probable cause," and may be intentionally disguised as an actual breach of the law, e.g., resisting arrest. Or in a stressful situation—say, a demonstration—certain actions seem more threatening to a policeman, or certain types of people seem more probably dangerous, and the police will book these people on fictitious charges and lie without qualm to support their action.

The cover charge for a crime that the officer knows has not been committed is justified as the elimination of a more serious threat, and outright fabrications of the truth are justified in a number of ways that are consistent with the police theory of eliminating dangers before they become even more serious.

All of these violations of the law by the police are rampant examples of official anarchy. They happen because policemen

have hatreds (like all of us), self-interests (like all of us), oper-
ate in personally dangerous situations (unlike all of us), and
overreact out of fear (like so many of us). Police anarchy is
understandable; but it is and should remain illegal. It can and
must be stopped by law and by vigorous law enforcement.

If only POGONOGO were on the job!

4

The Military
and Other Asylums

"They all belong to the syndicate," Milo
said. "And they all know that what's
good for the syndicate is good for the
country, because that's what makes
Sammy run. The men in the control
towers have a share, too, and that's why
they always have to do whatever they
can to help the syndicate."

Catch-22

Every society, infatuated by its own survival, maintains a force it dreams reasonably capable of defending its borders. No society ever protected itself for long against a determined invader by just talking to him or by refusing to talk to him. Diplomacy, silence, and passive resistance have minimal potential for dimming visions of pillage and rape of conquerors. And there is little reason, even in the nuclear age, to expect that they ever could. Such is the explanation for the ubiquity of armies, for the essence of militarism is the controlled utilization of the maximum force a society can muster as a deterrent against potential hostility, and as a defense once that rancor swells into war.

No society can maintain itself and continue its established ways unless its military is effective as first-line defender or as an avenger. So whatever a society is truly reflects the success or failure of its military. In this sense, what we are, we owe to our military. But though this is true, fears of invasion or destruction can preoccupy a society so much that it becomes little else but an armed camp. History records the existence of societies that became extensive bivouacs, governed by third-rate generals demanding the tight discipline of a forward artillery outpost. Many countries today, controlled by juntas of generals and colonels, also fit this blueprint for barely social living.

However, there is also a hoary tradition whereby the society demands a fundamental separation between the military and the state. In such societies, the military is demoted to being a lesser part of the social structure, and is run by the government. External defense is but one of many functions a society usually delegates to government.

In countries with a long history of such a separation, substantial stress frequently arises between the intelligentsia and the military. A famous French statesman, Georges Clemenceau, authored a perpetually popular lament of antimilitarists. It went something like: "War is too important to be left to the generals." We can rest assured that military men believe government is too important to be left to the politicians. Hence the mutual distrust among generals, statesmen, and intellectuals.

The American Constitution explicitly separates the state from the church in the Bill of Rights. Constitutional mention of the cleavage between the state and its military is less explicit. That is because in some ways they are inseparable, though divisible. In the first article of the Constitution, Congress is empowered to tax in order to maintain an army. That same power is implicitly left to the states as well. The so-called reserve clause empowers each state to maintain its militia, or, as it is called in contemporary America, the National Guard. The Constitution also allows individual Americans the right to take up cudgels themselves against invaders: that is the provision in the first amendment allowing individual citizens the right to "maintain arms." Thus, the basic law of the United States does not give even the federal or state military exclusive domain over the society's external defense. Such is the depth of American suspicion and jealousy of any public monopoly of force, and the result was an attempt to guarantee the diffusion and limitation of military power in America. It succeeded almost too well.

For example, late-1930's newsreels on U.S. Army training procedures revealed ragtag groups of sad sacks, brandishing broomsticks instead of rifles, and pretending close-order drill. This was a fair picture of America's "preparedness" against enemy attack as late as 1939, and an accurate gauge of the limited prestige and respect Americans reserved for their military up to that time. Little was spent on the military, and, with a quaint sense of equity, Americans allowed the military to expend little for them. The Second World War changed all that drastically.

72

The emergence of the cold war, so quick on the heels of the United States' most panoramic hot war, created a fresh "need" for a larger, if not bloated, peacetime military establishment. Despite the displacement of kitchen utensils by nuclear ones, America was sold on the unprecedented necessity to become a worldwide fortress—Columbia, armed to the teeth. Such was the burden of responsibility of the newly (and self-) proclaimed "leader of the free world."

The importance of the military in spending, respect, and political influence has risen at least proportionately since then, a fact noted by American War Hero Number One, Dwight D. Eisenhower, upon retiring from the Presidency. In perhaps the only statement Eisenhower ever made that excited the intellectual community, he cautioned his presidential successors against the sinister menace of an insatiable "military-industrial complex." Eisenhower seemed to express a fear that the military would gain a disproportionate share of power in internal and external political American affairs: economic, social, and political. His apparent concern was that the traditional lines between the military and state would become blurred or, worse still, wiped out. The problem was that in our "new industrial state"—with its heavy ante in the world order of things and with a believable threat from a blustering, nuclear-tipped, and seemingly implacable enemy, the military had to have a much larger say in what things should be done, and how.

The degree of power and influence the military possesses in any political system is measured by the amount of its society's natural and human resources directly and indirectly allotted by and to the armed forces. In other words, we must ascertain how much influence or control the military has, directly or indirectly, in the production and location of goods and services. For the military itself manufactures nothing and exists mainly to distribute waste and at least potential destruction, which is justified in terms of self-defense or living room.

In societies that separate it from political control, the military is a branch of the bureaucracy, largely confined to carrying out policies made by the politicos. However, we know that all administrators actually engage in extensive policy making at lower and middle levels of responsibility. And so it is with the military, particularly as our bureaucracy and military establishment grow, and as long as the foreign threat to our national security remains credibly frightening. Even at the highest levels of policy making (strategy), the military does and should wield substantial influence. After all, it has unique access to much relevant and critically important information, as well as the exclusive support of a large concentration of experts on matters of strategic defense. It is right and proper that its influence be felt throughout the society in policy making at all levels.

What's the problem, then? Well, the military is as directly subject to Parkinson's Law as are other components of bureaucracy. The military hierarchy, like any other, tends to generate extra work for itself, exhibiting the familiar bureaucratic inclination to expand wherever room can be found, created, or made to seem to exist. Some people think the military is the apotheosis of this "creeping crud," but that remains to be proved.

Next, being a bureaucracy, the military is directly subject to the tenets of the Peter Principle, which teaches us that executive incompetence tends to find and inhabit its own level. What this means is that bureaucrats strive for promotion and do move up as long as they do a good job. When they get to a position that is beyond their skills or interest, they tend to do a bad job and thus fail. Then they are not promoted—and stay at that level doing a poor job. Whether the military is the leading example of creeping Peterism, as others claim, also remains to be proved.

That a fattened military has eaten its way into the key policy-making pantries in American society, then, may well be a function of our bureaucratic obesity, normal subconscious, self-service, and Peterism. Although alarming, it is theoretically checkable, if not reversible. Certainly, there is no taint of lawlessness about it—in itself—even though it erodes the base of our traditional wall against military ingress to national political power.

But there is also a problem of illegal military encroachments into areas traditionally forbidden to the military. Whether President Eisenhower had this in mind too is immaterial, as the reality and enormity of the incursions exist anyway.

First, there is possible intentional, or wantonly negligent, misrepresentation of defense "needs" in terms of the political and strategic situation abroad. Second, there is very possible intentional or recklessly negligent misrepresentation of procurement costs of military hardware (and software) for those "needs." It seems obvious that the military has peculiar ways of perceiving the world and a rigid set of national priorities at increased variance with those of some other members of the American power elite. These are strongly held values, capable of influencing the military's judgment so as to distort realities.

One problem of military lawlessness occurs when the military realizes that its priorities are different, and lies outrightly, suppresses data, or selectively publicizes its "truth," with the consequence that it gains a larger and larger share of the policymaking pie than it deserves. This is the real gravity of the disclosures by Senator William Proxmire (D-Wis.), among others, on the fantastic cost overruns on so many military projects, including the C-5A. It is almost a national joke these days, but it is no laughing matter. For we are not dealing only with what certainly seems to be intentional underestimating of costs by a military-industrial axis. It is also an intentional gain of power at the expense of our civilian polity, and against our fundamental law.

When military expansion into policy making occurs as a result of active or passive fraud, or when laws are broken or ignored which have the effect of accomplishing this (personal conflict of interest), then we have military anarchy—an especially treasonous crime against the American nation-state. Those who perpetrate such crimes should be held responsible in that context rather than in any less reprehensible one. So what is said to be liberal rhetoric against the military-industrial complex is actually a conservative viewpoint.

This is also the case with another recently disclosed military venture into civilian life that smells suspiciously like another intentional invasion into areas heretofore and legally off limits to military men.

THE ONUS OF CONUS?

Fort Holabird, Maryland, is the hub of the United States Army intelligence program, where the Army has bred many of its agents in a cozy, college-campuslike atmosphere. Holabird has also long been a repository for mountains of military intelligence information. What constitutes legitimate military information, however, should become a perennial subject for the National Forensic League.

A more conservative opinion maintains the perhaps outdated notion that military information should be confined to foreign enemies, certain and potential. The Army, at least nowadays, collects much more information than that, for it now has a new military-intelligence infatuation with American citizens, and it has nothing to do with any conventional foreign war. These new objects of military interest need not have been in the United States Army, be in it presently, nor have broken any laws.

According to conventional and traditional concepts of American government, the internal police power is the legal province of state and local authorities, whose function it is to ensure local order throughout the United States. There is no national police in America. The FBI and T-men have some nationwide police power, but this is restricted to federal crimes, though federal police agencies do cooperate with local police on a variety of matters.

The United States Army has no general local police authority, while various state National Guards have little. Should emergencies arise, like the Civil War or widespread urban rioting, then the American Army can be called upon to restore domestic tranquillity. But this has been a very rare occurrence in America, partially because civil authorities are aware of the risk in turning over police powers to the military. Each small step in that direction is a leap toward the garrison state; it is much easier to turn an Athens into a Sparta than a Sparta into an Athens.

But after the urban riots of the middle and late sixties—and some widely publicized gibberish about "urban guerrilla warfare"—the Intelligence Section of CONUS (Continental U. S. Army Command) began to and may still continue to gather and store much data on the personal lives and lawful political activities of a large number of American citizens. This number includes, according to some ex-intelligence officers, the rank-and-file membership of such wild-eyed organizations as the American Civil Liberties Union and the National Association for the Advancement of Colored People.[1] According to a 1971 estimate, the Army has spied on 18,000 Americans from 1967 to 1969.[2] *Life* magazine estimated that the Army has hoarded "millions of dossiers" on "persons of interest" (including ordinary writers of letters to editors, businessmen, and birth control advocates).[3]

Americans have become familiar with the activation of Army units for a variety of domestic police missions since the Korean War. President Eisenhower sent the National Guard to Little Rock, and President Kennedy sent them to Oxford, Mississippi.

National Guard units have been assigned to a variety of pacification patrols. Some of us living in Detroit were relieved to learn that George Romney, then governor of Michigan, had ordered the National Guard into the area two days after the assassination of Martin Luther King. We had been evicted from our cups of coffee in the Wayne State University cafeteria by an organized group of blacks the day before, and forced off the street by several hundred black high school students shortly thereafter. It was a tense situation. So the troops came in and imposed a curfew, and everyone was confined to quarters from 8 P.M. to the next morning for ten straight days. Although it was depressing to sit inside and listen to armored personnel carriers and jeeps clank through the streets night after night, it cooled the situation with no loss of life or limb to anyone in Detroit.

Since the Army proved effective as a local keeper of the peace in the past, it is reasonable for it to anticipate a future in municipal pacification. Because of this potential call to colors, the military deems essential its occasionally irresistible penchant for seeking and keeping information on private citizens. One Major General, as late as 1971, called it the military's "right to intelligence," arguing that "in 1967 and 1968 urban riots ravaged some American cities. The Army was called out to support civil authority. Just as the police must maintain information about people and forces which constitute a danger to public order, any agency assuming police responsibility must have the information essential to the performance of its task." [4]

The general contends, in other words, that the military has a need to know. He is wrong. For the Army to enter into spying on private citizens, it must be far more persuasive in demonstrating such a need. Only unqualified necessity could justify breaching the traditional and legal American insulation of the Army from such internal-police political intelligence. For despite the general's justification of the Army's being summoned again for policing, there is no suggestion that the necessary intelligence cannot be competently garnered by established federal agencies, including the CIA and FBI, as well as by state and city police departments. Furthermore, there has been no audible complaint by Army officials that they were denied such pertinent information by local officials during the urban riots or that their operations were hampered by any incompleteness in the intelligence they requested.

Aside from the frivolous and expensive duplication of information about well-known radicals, this activity has amounted to a clear intrusion on the political freedoms of the broader American political community. It was a gigantic stride toward Big Brotherism in direct opposition to any concept of a free and open society. The Supreme Court of the United States recently forbade some governmental practices that had a "chilling effect" on freedom of speech. Can the CONUS computer do less than send sub-zero shivers through freedom of speech and assembly, as well as freedom of the press?

Late in 1970, there were several disclosures about Army spying on some prominent American political leaders, including some well-known nonradicals like Adlai Stevenson III. The ACLU filed suit on the matter and elicited further evidence from former intelligence agents that the New Action Army was deeply involved in internal intelligence work. Little did we know how "new" our new army was.

The federal judge dismissed the case and refused to enjoin the Army from its new hobby because he felt such "Keystone Kops" activities were no serious threat to American political freedom. But who ever said it had to be serious? First stages of syphilis may not be serious either, but it would be unwise to dismiss it as a bad case of pimples. The point is that there was no justification presented—or possible—for such behavior by the responsible Army officers. They had entered into a civilian police activity without showing that the civilian authorities were incompetent to gather the relevant and essential intelligence.

Further disclosures in March, 1972, showed that Army surveillance was even more widespread than had been believed; it included many middle-of-the-road U.S. Senators and Governors. Doing this knowingly and willingly was in itself a serious violation of our fundamental law, and the fact that it was bungled in no way forgives it or makes it funny. The source of these revelations, Senator Sam Ervin (Dem.-S.C.), found his own name on some of the Army's domestic-spying records. I doubt that it tickled him pink.

A second facet to the military anarchy inherent in this situation was the knee-jerk response of high military officials to deny categorically that any such spying was being conducted by the Army. If they had reason to believe otherwise, then they were intending to mislead the public on an important issue. But subsequent revelations of the fact and extent of military domestic spying indicate that the denials were willful attempts to cover up the truth. There was also a good deal of evidence at the C-5A hearings that some military men had tried to intimidate key witnesses and falsify evidence. Such actions would be direct violations of law prohibiting interference with congressional hearings. Military misrepresentation to the public, or to the public through the mass media, is equally dangerous to the public interest and to the public's right to control its military, and are violations of the military's obligation to refrain from overstepping its lawful bounds. This should be made a high public crime.

What is the onus of CONUS? It is to keep itself out of internal police work. What is the burden of the military? It is to realize that it can be a more effective subversive agent than any the FBI might pursue. But modern life, modern technology, and international realities being what they are and promise to be, there seems little hope that we can expect the military to understand this without a threat of heavy sanctions for their misunderstanding it.

THE NATIONAL GUARD AS COSSACKS

But sometimes military zeal to guard the ramparts of America does more than threaten civilian rule or civilian freedoms. For example, the National Guard managed to earn a very bad name for itself in a very short time. The fact that the Guard is an Army unit, trained as soldiers and not as police, fails to absolve it from responsibility for the police anarchy it commits in the name of law enforcement. In defense of the Guard, let it be said that its appearances came in times of great distress, that it was faced by bitter enmity, often not of its making, and that it was, at the time, ill trained to meet the particular problems it was called upon to redress. And there is not too much reason to believe that things would be different in the future.

Like some of their compatriots in blue, though, the National Guardsmen have fostered maxibrawls and (National Guard) riots, and they have acted out cold contempt of court, at least regarding judicial notions of the civil rights of American citizens.

The Newark and Detroit riots of 1967 occasioned numerous instances when National Guardsmen were responsible for crimes against person and property. Some members of the Guard believed they had free rein to machine-gun residences and conduct "reconnaissance by fire" into crowds, particularly when they reached the limit of their tolerance for verbal abuse, or felt they were in some degree of danger of physical harm to themselves.

The usual official justification for leaning on the trigger has been "sniper fire," but almost all independent official and semi-official investigations indicate that the Guard's rifle response was well beyond what was reasonably necessary, even granting that someone under fire might overreact. There was so much gratuitous rifle fire in Newark from Guard units that they sometimes were warring with one another.

Furthermore, according to the New Jersey Governor's Select Commission, which investigated the Newark riot, there was "evidence of prejudice against Negroes, during the riot" by National Guardsmen that "resulted in the use of excessive and unjustified force and other abuses." [5] The commission also found that "some national guardsmen" participated in property damage against the Negro community in Newark by smashing windows designated with the sign SOUL BROTHER. Since black looters had spared them, and had broken only windows of white store owners, some guardsmen decided to equalize wrongs. It was a heavy touch of khaki anarchy.

What happened in Plainfield, New Jersey, was worse, as the Guard performed in a quasi-martial law situation (the governor had proclaimed the area to be in a "state of disaster"). A search of the black community for some few dozen missing M-1's (stolen from an armory) resulted in widespread bullying and a random destruction of personal property. The size and style of the operation seemed aimed at punishment and intimidation rather than at retrieving a few weapons.

As one observer noticed, it made little sense for armed troops to capsize drawers and ransack containers far too small to hold the missing weapons, even if they were field-stripped. It made little sense to use heavy armored equipment. The black residents of Plainfield probably find it difficult even today to think of the United States Army as their very own.

Accounts of what has happened from time to time on college campuses under the supervision of police and military units sound like the Hollywood version of the old-time protection rackets. The Kent State episode is particularly instructive in this regard. For instance, there can be little doubt that the National Guard units at Kent State were harried and abused by many students, particularly the more radical organizers of the demonstrations. But their claim of self-defense is indefensible in light of the fact that the four youngsters shot to death were themselves innocent of presenting any imminent physical threat to the Guardsmen. Some of the victims were even passers-by. Several soldiers obviously fired haphazardly into an unarmed crowd and were therefore guilty of voluntary manslaughter, if not outright murder. Even had there been sniper fire, there was no evidence that it came from the direction of the crowd that was riddled by bullets.

In late July 1970, the Department of Justice released a memorandum on the Kent State tragedy. It was based on data gathered by more than one hundred FBI agents in and around the Kent area, including extensive interviewing of guardsmen present during the shootings. The memorandum declared that the guardsmen were "not surrounded by demonstrators and could have controlled the situation without shooting had they made arrests and used tear gas, which they still had despite using part of their gas supply earlier." The memorandum went on to note,

"No guardsman was injured by flying rocks or projectiles and none was in danger of his life at the time of the shooting." The memo concluded, in light of this information, that the killings were "unnecessary."

Granting the truth of the memorandum, there is reason to suspect motivation other than fear and self-defense behind the volley of bullet fire into a crowd of defenseless American students. Could there have been resentment and hatred? Given the objective lack of danger, it seems probable enough to support a thorough investigation of the six guardsmen singled out by the Justice Department as the killers. But these six may only be the tip of the iceberg, and, from the official attempts to whitewash this action, one could conclude that this sort of hostile feeling ran through a large part of the Ohio National Guard, from top to bottom, and perhaps through other Guard units as well.

For instance, let's take a look at what happened around the same time in Albuquerque, at the University of New Mexico (UNM). This incident enjoyed a short-lived, low visibility since there were no fatalities. But in a way it seems more shocking, as there was much less cause to occasion any bloodshed.

The Cambodian invasion and the Kent State affair had their impact among the students of UNM, which included moderates as well as liberals and radicals. As at so many other schools, UNM students managed to "liberate" some campus space from authority to show the extent of their concern. The university was ordered closed by the governor, partly in reaction to a few violent incidents among the students during the dawn of the New Mexico demonstrations. A scheduled conference of state governors in Albuquerque was also canceled because of potential violence, and the governor ordered the National Guard to stand by for an appearance on the UNM campus.

One of the salient issues was the occupation of the Student Union Building by student strikers. The students were already in defiance of an ultimatum from the president of the university to leave, and they were in immediate danger of having a court tell them to vacate. Moreover, there were strong community pressures to have the police expel the students, with or without the help of the Guard.

The pot was about to boil, but there was still a lid of hope. For one thing, the university president was still negotiating with the students. While the negotiations were still in progress, the local police entered the campus and began to rout the students. Happily, it was a reasonably gentle "bust." Soon the Student Union was completely reliberated by the police with only token resistance from the students. So far, so good: mission accomplished—no violence.

But with five hundred onlookers and sympathizers still milling about the outside of the building, the National Guard juggernaut rolled onto the campus in a convoy of trucks. Some three hundred strong, they leaped from the trucks, and with no reported provocation, fixed bayonets to the tips of their rifles. What was to happen was surreal. I quote the *Village Voice* at this point:

> A column of 60 men began moving up toward the front of the [Student Union Building], facing a group of students and newsmen gathered on a mall divided in the center by a row of huge, circular concrete flowerpots.
>
> Suddenly the Guardsmen marching forward between the building and the flowerpots began running toward the students, their bayonets lowered at the students' backs. Billy Norland, the Albuquerque television newsman, raised his camera in front of the Guardsmen, yelling "Press! Press!" as they advanced. His camera had the station's call letters across the front, but Guardsmen didn't seem to notice. One stabbed him in the chest and knocked him to the ground. Another stabbed him again, yelled at him, and stabbed him a third time. . . .
>
> Another newsman standing near Norland was stabbed in the arm as he ran to the cameraman. A student running from the Guardsmen tripped; a Guardsman caught up with him, put a bayonet blade in his shoulder and told him not to move,

then leaned on his rifle and pushed the blade two inches into his back.

According to the report in the *Village Voice*, eleven persons were stabbed. One student "will not use a leg again."

Student radicals, ex-student radicals, and faculty radicals are well cued to the tendency of National Guard units, as well as of local policemen or sheriffs, to overrespond on college campuses. They know their protests have large numbers of close sympathizers, and that this combination attracts larger numbers of semisympathizers, enemies, and the fascinated. They know that demonstrations will persist because America's problems will not be solved quietly. They know, too, that $P + M \times P = GA$. In other words, (1) profanity, plus (2) minor injuries inflicted on police or military, times (3) phony sniper fire (dropping some loud firecrackers), equals *haphazard overreaction* (government anarchy).

Military anarchy can be a hail of gunfire into large clusters of students or into student residences, a gas attack from helicopters that poisons the surrounding community, or a charge of Cossacks into hundreds of children and newsmen. Military massacres and mayhem are something we can do without. It is a fearful outbreak of lawlessness that is no less harmful to our system of law and order because the anarchists are clad in government issue.

MALEXPENDITURES

I don't wish to spend much time on Vietnam, that is, on the issue of to what degree it was a military-instigated policy or a military disregard of its legal international responsibilities. Among other problems, the stated political and military objectives in Vietnam have been very, very vague from the beginning, and there are numerous difficulties in penetrating the real meaning of America's involvement there.

On the other hand, every so often some atrocity catches the public eye which, if it turns out to be true, demonstrates military behavior clearly beyond what the Army can legally do, even in combat. The infamous My Lai slaughter was a splendid example of how euphemisms disguise true high military policy and a splendid picture of certain double standards of morality inherent in American military justice. There, an American Army company managed to reduce a South Vietnamese village populated by the halt, lame, pregnant, and infantile to a mass graveyard. It was certainly a massacre to equal the well-publicized Nazi destruction of Lidice in Czechoslovakia in the Second World War. There seems to be no reasonable doubt that the My Lai episode was a clear case of American military lawlessness, a gross violation of international law. According to the principles established at the Nuremberg war crimes trials, a soldier is guilty of murder if he kills unarmed women and children, even if ordered to do so. The courts-martial against a group of enlisted men and junior officers recognized this and did their best to apply it. In this regard, the military is to be commended.

But My Lai raised similar questions about other policies, like the "free-fire zone" policy in Vietnam, according to which inhabited, nonbelligerent villages and other areas were targeted for eventual bombing simply because they were in "Vietcong-controlled" territory. Euphemism aside, this meant that American warplanes were to drop unexpended ordnance on anyone or anything moving in these wide areas of rural South Vietnam because the territory was classified as being under NLF control. That didn't mean that all or even most residents were Vietcong or VC supporters. Is it less criminal to kill innocent civilians by bombing? Is a bomb less obnoxious than a bullet? Not to the corpse.

Then there was the military policy known as "reconnaissance by fire." What this meant was that a patrol was told it could shoot into a village. If anyone returned the fire, the village would be considered supportive of the Vietcong or under its control. Consequently, air attacks with bombs and napalm could be summoned to pulverize "the enemy." But if someone shot into your town, wouldn't shooting back be an act of self-defense rather than a consequence of the Communist Manifesto? Obviously this policy took a heavy toll on noncombatants, including innumerable innocent women and children. And it was probably quite intentional. It made good sense to a military fighting such an unconventional war; it was a policy most likely designed to dry up the "sea of people" in which all guerrilla forces presumably swim. It had to be a high-command policy, emanating from the top.

These were policies executed in the name of the American people. Yet they were policies unannounced to the American people, camouflaged by a jargon that could easily deceive the American people but not the peasants in South Vietnam, who understood napalm, not English. A former U.S. prosecutor at Nuremberg, Brigadier General (Ret.) Telford Taylor (presently a law professor at Columbia University), has stated:

> The by now voluminous reportorial literature on the Vietnamese war leaves little doubt that air strikes are routinely directed against hamlets and even single habitations . . . , in reliance on information of varying reliability. Obviously, these tactics are a response to the nature of guerrilla warfare, and the difficulty of sifting out the "enemy" in a society where there are many shades of inimical activity, and friend and foe are not readily distinguishable. Making full allowance for these difficulties, however, it is clear that such reprisal attacks are a flagrant violation of the Geneva Convention on Civilian Protection, which prohibits "collective penalties" and "reprisals against protected persons," and equally in violation of the Rules of Land Warfare. Son My, after all, was suspected of harboring the Vietcong, and if (as has been seen) it was nonetheless a war crime to round up inhabitants and shoot them without trial, it would be equally criminal to have killed them by a surprise air attack.[6]

Taylor went on to suggest that if the Nuremberg principle

87

were strictly enforced, General William Westmoreland could be prosecuted as a war criminal for carrying out, if not recommending, these policies, among others.

The accusing finger could point even higher—to the pinnacle of civilian government. Such could be the legal consequences of policies so reckless in the expenditure of human life. Surely it also demonstrates the double standard in America's system of military justice in prosecuting the Sergeant Mitchells, the Lieutenant Calleys, and the Captain Medinas, while bypassing the brass and that component of our political elite that established similar policies from the war's very beginning. And let us not forget that these same policies are *still* being carried out today in Vietnam, Cambodia, and Laos.

Of course none of these pogrom programs were directed against Americans. It is not the kind of internal "government lawlessness" with which this book is mainly concerned. But we might ponder the damage it has done to America as an ideal, and to American soldiers as human beings.

Another type of Vietnam incident, one that was and probably remains a direct military crime against our own society, is the clear violation of explicit and clearly legal military and political directives.

In the autumn of 1970, the same fellow who broke the My Lai story was again in Vietnam, this time on a different assignment. Donald Ridenhour, newly a freshman newspaper correspondent, was visiting American headquarters in Chu Lai, where he uncovered evidence that the American Army was dumping tons and tons of a chemical defoliant called Orange. Until this disclosure, military officials had been denying similar charges. This time, however, admissions were forthcoming.

What is most significant is that in the spring of 1970, several federal agencies including the Departments of Agriculture and HEW had finally prevailed on military and civilian officials to terminate defoliation by the use of this agent. The reason? There was substantial proof that this chemical would cause birth defects in humans. So Deputy Defense Secretary David Packard, after due consultation with his superiors, banned the use of it after April 25, 1970. That, coming from a top government official, was the law of the land.

But certain military officials, top men in the Americal Division in Vietnam, decided that Orange was better in the trees than in the can. This was a malappropriation of government property, and a misexpenditure of taxpayers' property, both subject to court-martial. There was no mention of any such action pending.

In any event, the military malexpenditure of life and money in Vietnam is becoming more and more evident, and the picture of American military lawlessness there clearer. Most of what happened there is still well within any statute of limitations on prosecution.

One aftermath of the Korean War was a witch-hunt known as the McCarthy era. It was based on the idea that America had been sold out in Korea. It may well be that one consequence of the Vietnam War will be another investigation into another alleged sellout of American ideals. This time there is much more hard empirical evidence to support that charge. This time the prosecutors of the charge will be of a liberal persuasion. This time the procedures must adhere to due process of law, because it was that, if anything, that was sold out.

The military establishment is in many ways a government unto itself; it is, to the American citizen who is recruited into its ranks, a microcosm of all governmental functions. It has a prosecutorial system, courts, and prisons, just like governments elsewhere. But, unlike many governments in the world, it is a nearly total dictatorship, and its court and prison systems have long reflected this fact, prompting another Clemenceau observation that enjoys wide circulation: "Military justice is to justice as military music is to music."

Some think Clemenceau gave it too much credit. For the lack of connection between justice and military justice may go deeper.

As commentators have noted, the purpose of the system of military justice is not to work justice; it is to impress discipline, the rugged discipline the military thinks necessary to carry out its mission. This makes life inside the military like that in any "total institution," or what one noted sociologist has called an asylum.[7]

However, I do not wish to pick a lengthy fight with the Code of Military Justice, or to rant against the concept of trial the military maintains. I would rather refer the reader to Robert Sherrill's recent book,[8] and his persuasive argument that the Army has long violated the canons of constitutionality, with the advice and consent of our civilian court system. For instance, it is staggering to learn that at general courts-martial, the commander still chooses the prosecutor, the members of the jury (officers under his command), the military defense officer, and the jury itself decides on objections from defense counsel as to bias in the jury membership. Shouldn't American soldiers be entitled to a fair trial? Where in the Bill of Rights does it say that an American citizen loses his inalienable rights once he agrees to serve his country in the military?

Since the Supreme Court and other lawmaking institutions have traditionally approved this, I leave such questions aside and will touch instead on more directly obvious outlawry practiced under the system of military justice—that in the military prisons. This is a more cleanly cut example of military violation of laws that even our civilian courts would have to condemn, if the facts were presented. It is not a debatable question of unconstitutionality, but a fact of illegality.

Allegations and more allegations are being laid at the foot of the military establishment about the horrendous conditions in its stockades and brigs. In the last few years, repeated and nauseating revelations have surfaced describing what happens in these compounds at Fort Dix, the Presidio, Camp Pendleton, and others. Reports range from making soldiers take showers and then stand naked in winter weather for hours,[9] to handcuffing marines in a spreadeagle position, their feet dangling above the ground, and then subjecting them to prolonged beatings.[10] They include the grossest tales of sadism, like this one at Fort Dix:

> [I] saw this prisoner being taken to segregation. He was being hit on top of the head when all of a sudden he let one go and landed on Sgt. ———'s face. . . . Then they really put it to him. . . . He was in the straps about five or six hours. He was laid on a bunch of boards about eight inches off the ground and every thirty minutes or so he was picked up and let fall hitting his head and abdomen, each time from higher up . . . his face was bashed up. . . .[11]

They include the story of Private Richard Bunch, at the Presidio, who told a guard, after refusing an order, to "be sure to aim for my head." The guard complied, and Bunch lost his head, to a shotgun blast. Prisoners who staged a sit-down demonstration to protest Bunch's murder, as well as the alleged commission of innumerable acts of brutality and sadism, were all tried and convicted of the famous Presidio Mutiny. Some got sentences (for this "nonviolent mutiny") of up to fifteen years in prison! [12]

The charges mount without end. In fact, ex-Senator Charles Goodell of New York and Senator Alan Cranston of California reported in 1970 that complaints from no fewer than twelve military prisons were clogging their desks. And if military prison brutality is more unthinkable than that in the civilian prisons, it could be because military prison guards are rarely trained for their jobs. According to Karl Punnell, writing in the *Nation,* neither the commanding officer of the Presidio nor any of the guards had "any training for penal work." Most of the time, according to him, young MP's have a blunderbuss thrust into their hands and are ordered to stand guard. Defense Department Instruction No. 1325.4 says: "Personnel . . . shall be specifically trained in the control, management and correction of persons." This is but one other military violation of rules, regulations, and common sense, another instance of official disregard for official mandates which results in lethal damage to Americans and America.

But military dungeons are not the only enclaves in America in which Americans are treated inhumanely as a matter of due course. There are other asylums from America within America, the most obvious being the prisons and penitentiaries.

BEYOND CRUEL AND UNUSUAL PUNISHMENT

Someone once observed that you can judge a society by the way it treats its prisoners. If that's so, few can swell with pride. In many societies, no bones are made about it. A prisoner disappears; goodbye.

But in America, it is different. According to its "modern" laws and enlightened penal theories a man who goes to prison should be "rehabilitated," that is, refitted and retooled so that he can be a "productive" citizen when he returns home. In other words, Americans maintain "correctional" institutions, at least according to law.

If that is what prisons are supposed to be doing, they are doing a remarkably rotten job of it, because America's recidivism rate is unconscionably high. Most prisoners, after winning their freedom, quickly recapture their unfreedom. The main reason is obvious: the prisons are not geared for reform, they are programed for dehumanizing storage. Americans say it is other than that, but in truth, the manifest function of the prisons is to keep prisoners in a dismal depot, ill clad, ill housed, ill fed, and ill treated (who wants to spend good tax money on bad eggs?).

So it is hardly astonishing that if someone doesn't enter prison with a hardened criminal mentality, he will probably emerge with one. What is worse, most Americans still refuse to cope with the fact that it is so bad. Even when it is admitted, little if anything is done.

Libraries bulge with criminology and penology books that

make recommendation upon recommendation about how to make prisons more rehabilitative. There is talk about better construction of buildings and more rational layouts for the cells, making them less depressing, for example. There is talk of getting better guards, ones trained to being "correctional" rather than "punitive." There is even liberal gossip about restoring married prisoners to their conjugal rights, that is, letting their wives pay them a real visit. There is the annual talk about financing far superior vocational programs in the jails, allowing prisoners to feel they are learning something of use to them (in a legitimate sense) once they get out.

But if one looks hard and long, one will rarely find even a passing hint about the everyday dehumanization generously served to prisoners by prison guards, other prison personnel, and favored or feared inmates with the full knowledge if not sanction of the prison staff. Inmates not only lose their civil rights, they forfeit their humanity.

In New York City, for example, there has been a new rash of exposés, mainly because the political activities of many intellectuals have led to the streets, and thence to jail. One recent book—entitled *Hellhole* [13]—centered on the House of Detention for Women of New York City. The book is the odyssey of two Bennington College girls arrested on a minor charge in 1965.

The girls were kept virtually incommunicado for three days, the prison guards insisting they couldn't telephone their lawyer during a holiday. (Irony of ironies, the holiday happened to be Washington's Birthday.) Furthermore, "homosexuality is increasingly aggressive. Girls were constantly making love with each other in front of the policewoman. I was in a situation where girls were constantly touching me and caressing me and sticking their hands between my legs." [14]

Among other documented items was the degrading and physically abusive vaginal examinations conducted by the prison doctor. A vaginal examination for peace demonstrators? Let me quote from *Hellhole*:

93

The vaginal examination was really brutal. I know I was hurt by the brusque way the doctor thrust the instrument in me— I mean, literally physically hurt. And, as for the young kids— God, I'll never forget one little girl who couldn't have been over eighteen and might, in fact, have been less. She screamed quite loud and kept protesting that she was a virgin. And from her reaction, she quite likely was. She was absolutely panicky. Nobody made an attempt to comfort her or to explain the nature of the examination or to treat her with any gentleness. The reaction was laughter from the surrounding prisoners, from the guards who were present and even or especially from the doctor.[15]

Let us remember that the federal Constitution guarantees to American citizens that there be no "cruel and unusual punishment" in store for them while on loan to any of America's prisons.

But what happened in Greenwich Village was lean pickings compared to reports of routine in the Arkansas state system. The quality of torment devised for inmates and the quantity of alleged prison homicides during the past few decades finally surfaced in 1968 as a scandal of major proportions.

A former superintendent of the Arkansas state prison system, Tom Murton, described a contraption he found in one of that state's prisons (Tucker) when he took charge. Called the Tucker Telephone, it consisted of an electric generator that was part of an old crank-style telephone, with two dry-cell batteries wired to it. An inmate would be brought in, stripped, and strapped to a table, with electrodes attached to his penis and big toe. Then someone would turn the crank, causing electric current to be shot into the man's testicles. In keeping with the shocking hilarity of it all, some of the "telephone calls" were naturally "long distance." Murton hardly needed to inform us that "some men were literally driven out of their minds."[16] It is difficult to conceive of a more cruel or more unusual punishment, yet it was an official routine of lawlessness.

Evidence of a series of murders at one of Tucker's sister

prisons, Cummins, even more than the "telephone," raised the short-lived public outcry in 1968. Estimates of the number of murdered prisoners exceeded a hundred. Murton himself is convinced that numerous murders were committed there, three of which he is quite certain. He has accumulated a stack of affidavits from past inmates claiming many instances of multiple and macabre murder. Among them are the following:

> I saw six men shotgunned to death in the yard and taken out and buried in the field.
> The spinal meningitis epidemic of 1952 was a fraud. The prisoners were killed in the hospital and the prison doctor wrote it up as meningitis.
> I saw an inmate killed when barbed wire was wrapped around his neck and he was dragged across a field by a horse.
> I saw three men beaten to death with bats.

Murton has posted a standing offer to "make the documents available to any serious investigative group." [17]

Oh yes, Murton was appointed to the superintendency in 1967, but was fired in 1968. In 1969 he wrote that what still happens daily in the Arkansas prison system happens every day in all American states and all American cities. Despite *ad hoc* investigating committees and spasmodic pressures for instant reform, the fact is that our prisons dole out a generous diet of degradation and cruelty.

Some of the worst prison staff outlawry is reserved for special prisoners—those whom "the system" fears for political reasons. One of the most astonishing examples of a wide-screen, full-color, prison-guard maxibrawl came during the People's Park melees in Berkeley.

At one point during those clashes, some four hundred people were corralled by the Alameda sheriff's office, hustled into buses mobilized for the occasion, and trundled off to a nearby prison called Santa Rita. Actually it wasn't a prison; it was a Rehabilitation Center by designation. But for those four hundred or so American citizens—college students, professors, housewives—for an objectively short, but subjectively interminable time, it was Dachau, albeit minus delousing, gas, and ovens.

The charges against the four hundred were relatively minor (unlawful assembly, disturbing the peace), which made it all the more outrageous for them to be forced to lie face down, motionless, on asphalt and gravel, for more than five hours in the broiling sun. Think of that: a five-hour bellyful of prison-yard asphalt and gravel on a hot, sunny California day. Lying there motionless, while guards walked up and down, administering an insult here, a threat there, here a poke, there a kick. Occasionally some guards would drag someone around a corner to "beat the living shit out of [him]." [18] The enormity of hatred in those guards that led to spasms of brutality and prolonged illegal harassment became near-legend in the Berkeley area. It was a bitter pen that scrawled on a Berkeley coffee-house wall: "Yes, Virginia, there really is a Santa Rita."

But frequently the harassment and brutality is not so quickly ended, nor so open to middle-class outrage.

One well-verified case of prison repression of black nationalists came to light in the spring of 1970, when Judge Constance Baker Motley, a Federal District Court judge in New York City, censured certain practices of Warden Harold Follett against an inmate named Martin Sostre. It might be noted that Sostre was no stranger to court. In fact, he was a diligent and daring jail-house lawyer.

One day a few years ago, he was summoned to the warden's office. On the warden's desk was a letter Sostre had written to his attorney. In the envelope were several legal documents Sostre had drafted to assist his lawyer with the case. The warden asked Sostre if he was licensed to practice law in New York. Sostre said no. The warden also asked him about several references Sostre made in the letter about a militant black nationalist group (Republic of New Africa). Sostre declined to answer, saying it was none of the warden's business. Because of his refusal to stop practicing cellblock law and to cooperate in the warden's interrogation, Sostre was forced to endure solitary confinement for over one year, and was liberated only by court order.

What was solitary like? The prisoner was confined to his cell for twenty-three hours a day. That one "free" hour was for "recreation" in a tiny, completely enclosed yard. Sostre refused this privilege because of the prerequisite physical exam—he would be forced to strip and submit to a rectal examination—before he could be admitted to that yard. He was not permitted to use the prison library, see movies, read newspapers, or work.

The day after his court-ordered release, by the way, he was found guilty of another prison crime and sentenced to solitude in his regular cell for several days. His crime? Dust on his cell bars. This happened on July 3, and as Sostre figured and the court so held, its purpose was to keep him from freely associating with his fellow prisoners during the Fourth of July celebration.

Judge Motley believed that this punishment and harassment was a deliberate attempt by a state official to intimidate a man for his holding and expressing hostile political beliefs. Although there may be cases in which a warden might be wise in isolating a troublemaker, there is law that prohibits prison officials from confining a man to solitary imprisonment for interminable periods. It is the constitutional stricture against cruel and unusual punishment.

Every once in a while someone in power sees the whole mess through a clear lens and refuses to go along with it. For instance, within a six-month period in 1971, two judges, one in Virginia and one in West Virginia, handed down blanket indictments of prison life in their states. The Virginia judge, Robert R. Merhige, a Federal District Court judge, ruled that many practices in the penitentiaries added up to a denial of due process under the Fourteenth Amendment.[19] This included the usual listing of despicable tortures (chaining people to cell bars or keeping them in solitary for 266 days without ever having a hearing). Judge George R. Triplett, of the Circuit Court of West Virginia, considered the entire correctional system in his state to be "cruel and unusual punishment," and he refused to recommit a prisoner to finish out his term.[20]

So it goes on in detention homes, state penitentiaries, work farms, and junior concentration camps, from coast to coast. Even wiser prison officials feel gripped by futility. They know what goes on and realize that many factors contribute to the hideous state of prison affairs. The problem is that these factors won't just fade away, for they find sustenance in some values and attitudes of the whole society, its ways of doing things and not doing things. They flourish in a society where political leaders hear, but do not listen.

In December 1969 Bronx County district attorney Burton Roberts wired Governor Nelson Rockefeller about the "horrendous conditions" in one of the city's prison complexes. These included, as usual, the ordinary problems of packing prisoners into unbearable and illegal closeness, keeping most prisoners detained for intolerable and illegal periods of time before trial, a number of run-of-the-mill episodes of illegal guard brutality to inmates, and an incapacity (and illegal unwillingness) to stop sexual assaults by some inmates on other inmates. Despite repeated warnings, and reports of reports of reports, and admission upon admission of fault, the inevitable occurred: a major prison riot in the fall of 1970 at the Queens House of Detention in Long Island City. It was a major inmate offensive—with many guards held prisoner of riot.

But even with Mayor Lindsay on the scene, negotiating anxiously with the inmates and guaranteeing the safe conduct of those inmates who would surrender, and even under the glare of newsmen, news photographers, and television cameras, the guards could not contain their hatred. As those inmates who surrendered came out, they were clubbed and kicked by guards, who were waiting for them. Eight inmates had to be sent to Bellevue Hospital.

Pity the mayor, pity the D.A., pity the governor, and pity enlightened correctional officers. And pity the guards. But pity the prisoners the most. For American prisons are official asylums from the law, institutions beyond the most sordid nightmares of our founding fathers.

The recent (Attica, Rahway) and future (etc.) prison rebellions not only raise what have become almost tired questions about the decency promised in our fundamental charters (the Constitution), they also demonstrate how poorly educated our prison population has been—to have waited so long. And Attica also proved how viciously some government officials would overreact to such statements of despair and protest. As at Kent State, the only deaths were caused by government guns. There was no serious threat of escape, and lethal punishment was assured anyone who killed any official hostage. No, death was a punishment decreed, on the spot, by gubernatorial fiat as a response to understandable outrage against intolerable conditions—conditions perpetuated, directly and indirectly, by government.

Nevertheless, the military and the prisons are not alone as such asylums from the law, though they could be the worst in terms of the physical punishment they offer as daily fare. For mental anguish, while trampling on the civil rights of inmates, we also have our state mental institutions and our entire public school system. The former is the more obvious example; if one wants a picture of the squalid surroundings and squandered humanity, I might advise that he or she see a movie called *Titticut Follies,* which details the ways and means in 16 millimeters.[21]

As for the latter, I won't dwell on it. However, it seems clear enough, from a daily perusal of our press, that educational officials are making it more explicit than ever that our schools, whether in the deepest slum or the most celestial suburb, put a heavy emphasis on discipline—much more, in some cases, than on their academic topics. Apparently it matters not, to all too many, what is learned or not learned. And it matters too much what students wear, how they coif their hair, and whether they decide to voice their political viewpoints, symbolically or by political behavior.

Many school systems pass and maintain with military efficiency a series of regulations that make it mandatory for high school students, in particular, to conform to the locally dominant social and political codes. Nowhere in our federal or state constitutions is it written: "The student shall be deprived of all civil rights of American citizenry." But the practice is that way everywhere. Indeed it has prompted a recent book to be called *The Student as Nigger,* an interesting compendium on a number of these practices.[22]

Thus, although there is no legal elbow room for asylums from the law in America, there are too many of them. Our military seems dedicated to violating international law as well as our own constitutional framework. Its penchant for secrecy and for gathering intelligence, at home and abroad, has made what it knows a source of real concern to those anxious to keep the military in its proper legal place. Furthermore, there is nothing in our Constitution, since the end of the Civil War, that would allow any of our citizens to be treated as criminals, as is so often the case in our military and in our schools. And there is nothing in our Constitution that would allow our criminals to be treated as animals. But so it goes. On and on. And be assured that it continues.

Of course, POGONOGO could stop it—once and for all.

5

Bureaucratic
Anarchy

TRUSCOTT: I must ask you to remain where you are. No one is to leave without my permission.

McLEAVY: Why?

TRUSCOTT: When you disobey my orders, sir, you make my job doubly difficult.

McLEAVY: On what authority do you give orders?

TRUSCOTT: You'd be considerably happier if you allowed me to do my duty without asking questions.

McLEAVY: Who are you?

TRUSCOTT: I'm an official of the Metropolitan Water Board, sir, as I've already told you.

McLEAVY: But the Water Board has no power to keep law-abiding citizens confined to their rooms.

TRUSCOTT: Not if the citizens are law-abiding.

McLEAVY: Whether they're law-abiding or not the Water Board has no power.

TRUSCOTT: I don't propose to argue hypothetical cases with you, sir. Remain where you are till further notice.

McLEAVY: I shall take legal advice.

TRUSCOTT: That is as may be. I've no power to prevent you.

McLEAVY: I want to telephone my lawyer.

TRUSCOTT: I can't allow you to do that. It would be contrary to regulations. We've no case against you.

Act I, *Loot*, by Joe Orton

Just as most Americans make their only contact with courts at the trial level and not the Supreme Court, most Americans touch the executive branch at its lowest decision-making level, the bureaucracy and not the President. Citizens see real-life government as O'Brien the cop, Beazley the postman, the faceless customs clerk, and Portnoy the social worker, making the rounds of his sublimations.

Modern government is a series of banal, though necessary, functions, only one of which is law enforcement, despite its recent prominence around election time. Though the FBI might command great visibility and respect, average personal contacts with government are far less glamorous: outwaiting passport lines, outwitting income tax booklets, and outraging regulating agencies by demanding personal service *and* efficiency. Moreover, the main criticisms of government are at this level too, like grumbling about political science professors at the state university who spend more time in political agitation than in political regimentation.

But whatever Mr. Normalcy's touch with government bureaucracy, he should realize that it, like other aspects of the state in America, is sired by and swaddled in law. It is law that puts bureaucracy into business, and law that tells bureaucracy what is not its business. In America, bureaucracies are the progeny of politics, and, like all government, are supposed to answer to the people.

Each administrative agency in the American system was set up by some law passed by some legislature—Congress, a state senate, a city council. The inseminating law is the agency's "enabling act," so called because it allows the agency to carry out its mission, its reason for being. The legislature also informs the agency how it should accomplish its goals and provides the wherewithal.

The American system being what it is, there is also law that sets express and implicit limits on how the agency can behave, on which state and federal constitutional boundaries must not be crossed. The law giveth, but the law also restricteth. Administrators, wherever they proliferate, are bound by oath and law to keep within borders set for them by their political parents. They can play as vigorously as they like, but not outside their pens.

However, this metaphor, like all metaphors, has limitations, for the restraint on the child in his cell is rigid, tangible, and discrete. But laws—as restraints—are very flexible, oftentimes difficult to understand, and sometimes self-contradictory. Even if the bureaucrat is dedicated, loyal, and obedient, the law may fail to furnish adequate guidelines.

So when laws are amorphous or schizophrenic, administrative action may seem illegal or inconsistent. Attitudes, personality, and the dynamics of organizational behavior play critical parts in the wide differences in administration. The same law may be administered differently from state to state, from time to time in the same agency, by the same person, from person to person in the same agency at the same time, etc. This frustrating situation, sometimes seen by the public as discrimination, sometimes as injustice, and sometimes as incompetence, is due to the plain fact that different people in different agency situations simply see facts or law differently.

Disparities in administration are so commonplace, though, that there is constant agitation to do something about it. This consternation is compounded and reinforced by the plain fact that administrative sins happen all too often when the law is extremely clear. Sometimes it is hard to believe that a bureaucrat did not know that his action or inaction was outside the concrete limitation of his power and authority.

When citizens resent shabby treatment at the hands of a seemingly cold and impersonal agency, or talk about incorrect interpretation of the enabling act or the agency's own rules, they are griping about simple misadministration. That is a problem of official inefficiency and misorientation.

When bureaucrats act clearly beyond their authority, we have official officiousness, a far more serious and political problem— a problem in *mal*administration, the perversion of administration. Maladministration must not be confused with the to-be-expected distortion of laws which happens because men are human, not divine; because men commit errors, and flunk their ideals. Parkinson's Law and the bumbling obesity of power are not at issue here. There is a steep and critical line to be drawn between muddling through, messing up, and intentionally desecrating the law.

Obviously, it is never simple to determine that an administrator is premeditatedly violating his oath of office. For one thing, an administrator will rarely admit it—at least, on the record. For another, he would almost invariably deny it. He would probably go to great lengths to cover it up beforehand, obviating the need for denial or patch-quilt alibis.

Still, sometimes it is admitted. On other occasions, it can be readily inferred from a series of actions on the part of a single administrator in a single case, or by a cluster of circumstantial evidence. And there should be no more reluctance to accuse a government official of government anarchy than to accuse a private citizen of some other criminal act.

TOO MANY DO-BADDERS

Steven Waldhorn, formerly a research associate at the Institute of Law and Social Sciences at the University of California at Berkeley, presented a paper in New York at the American Political Science Association national convention in September 1969 in which he claims there is a tremendous outbreak of administrative lawlessness, particularly in the area of social welfare. Many social welfare bureaucracies, Waldhorn contends, have changed the nature of their mission fundamentally. As a matter of fact, they have changed the primary goals they are in business to reach. Of course, the *de jure* mission is the same, but the *de facto* mission was, and remains, all but unrecognizable. In other words, many welfare workers play a different ball game, and an illegal one. Do-goodism is, in truth, do-baddism.

Waldhorn believes there are three major reasons for this. First, although administrative goals may be formally agreed upon by a legislature, the real conflict is rarely resolved by the enabling act. Active cross-pressures remain both in and beyond the political sphere. To put it another way, there is a frequent lack of goal consensus to begin with.

Second, perhaps as a result of this unabating conflict, most agencies and programs in the social welfare field are underfinanced by legislatures. There is much too little money to get the mandated job done.

Third, unlike police work, misadministration and maladministration in social welfare have very low visibility, and, it might be noted, the victims are less aware of their victimization. When police abuse you you know it.

Two professors at Columbia University School of Social Work, Richard Cloward and Frances Fox Piven, have this to say about the problem:

> Public welfare systems are under the constant stress of conflict and opposition made only sharper by the rising costs to localities of public aid. And, to accommodate this pressure, welfare practice everywhere has become more restrictive than welfare statutes; much of the time it verges on lawlessness.[1]

Professors Cloward and Piven mention some examples of the "lawlessness" to which they refer: (1) the agency's failure to inform its clients of the rights available to them; (2) "intimidating and shaming" their clients sufficiently so they will not press their claims; and (3) "arbitrarily denying benefits to those who are eligible."

How is this done? One of the more complex and controversial examples of violating the civil rights of clients that Waldhorn discusses is enforcement by welfare agents of what is called the man-in-the-house rule. Briefly, according to this rule, if a woman is collecting Social Security benefits, she cannot have a man living in her house who might be paying some or all of her expenses. Naturally, this is not an extraordinary practice— poor women are understandably loath to tell their welfare agents about the visitation of some good fortune.

So some agencies adopt a procedure known as the "midnight welfare search," in which welfare agents stage an evening raid on suspicious apartments to uncover any man in residence. Just barge right in; the more abrupt the better. If the woman offers resistance at the door, as many believe is her right, it is common to threaten her that refusal to admit them might lead to "automatic" termination of benefits to her or her child.

It is, of course, also understandable that people whose lives are wrapped up in government hate to see government swindled. To the man in the office, his agency is out to do good for needy people, and with woefully insufficient funds for all in the first place, they see a crying need to pinch pennies. So when it seems possible that a recipient of that scarce commodity, welfare money, is being adequately supported, this person is considered a chiseler and there should be some way to expose that person's deceit. Consequently, it is not necessarily malicious, even though mischievous, to go crashing into apartments in the dead of the night. But some legal experts consider it quite illegal for welfare agents to do it. It can't be unintentional, and even the worst criminals have the constitutional protection of a search warrant. Surely a person on relief—at worst a minor embezzler—deserves no less.

So goes the argument. But Waldhorn could not know that six members of the U. S. Supreme Court would soon disagree with him and hold, late in 1970, that welfare money was, in fact, the government's down payment on a citizen's waiver of her rights to privacy in her own home (who ever heard of a poor person owning a castle?). In other words, it was determined that welfare workers could storm clients' abodes—under certain circumstances —to ferret out hidden lovers and to discontinue payments if refused entry.

Of course, this may prove to be less than an open invitation to more abusive and ungrounded expeditions, as some civil libertarians now fear. The Court has not granted unlimited license for welfare agents to invade all homes at their whim and may yet delimit the scope of probable cause and the nature and range of the search. That remains to be seen. It still seems that America's Constitution outlaws many of the more abusive procedures perpetuated in some midnight welfare forays that have not yet reached the Supreme Court's eyes and ears.

A sharper example of alleged bureaucratic lawlessness comes in the administration of the public housing acts, particularly in administrative attempts to shield housing projects from potentially harmful tenants.

If you were administering a housing project, knowing that some tenants like to cause physical damage, you too would be wary of introducing new troublemakers into the development. When possible, you would also try to purge the old ones. Not only would that make your job easier, protect you from criticism from above, as well as from political opportunists, but it would also promote the aims of your administration: a more harmonious and better maintained public housing unit.

However, one report from an NYU Law School public housing project noted that "the basis for turning down a family's application may be based on a report of 'antisocial' behavior from past landlords, neighbors, or social agencies." The report continued: "Information may be received from any source without verification. . . . No provision is made for informing the applicant of adverse information or of the criteria used by the Authority." [2]

It is commendable for administrators to be concerned over such problems. The difficulty arises when housing administrators deprive people of a right to live in public housing, when they are qualified to live there, on the basis of rumor and gossip, without a hearing. There is no legal basis for this nonprocedure and much legal basis to ensure that due process is called for. The problem of keeping undesirables out of public housing could be resolved legally with due process. Government officials obviously choose to resolve it otherwise, sometimes out of ignorance, sometimes intentionally. If the latter is the case, then we are into maladministration, and into official anarchy.

Denying people their right to live in public housing is not the only way codes are flouted by public housing officials. Stuart Nagel, past director of an OEO legal services program in central Illinois, wrote an article called "The Poor Want Law and Order, Too." [3] In it he informs us that many tenants are bitter in their accusations against officials for their lack of enforcement, as opposed to malenforcement, of public housing laws.

Nagel states that the cities of Champaign and Urbana, Illinois, have laws scheduling fines of up to two hundred dollars per day for certain violations of housing codes, once it is determined that a violation exists. He then presents two revealing facts: (1) "Approximately 60 percent of the houses in the Champaign urban renewal area were found to have serious housing code violations, and 10 percent were so bad they were beyond feasible rehabilitation." (2) Yet a fine had "almost never" been levied "for housing code violations in Champaign County."

On the basis of these facts, it certainly appears that earnest and honest enforcement of the codes was lacking, again raising the specter of administrative lawlessness. For administrative sins of omission are nonetheless as pernicious as administrative sins of commission. Such a dramatic discrepancy should have provided ample excuse for investigation to find out why so little has been done. Naturally, it did not.

The administration of welfare or housing laws is hardly the only place where one finds hefty doses of administrative anarchy, virulent or dormant. And overzealousness, self-righteousness in administration, and lack of funds are not the only conceivable underlying causes.

STRICT CONSTRUCTIONISTS

During the autumn of 1969, America witnessed a series of protests in several major cities, organized to highlight one of America's most persistent problems: black unemployment and the craft unions' role in keeping black men down. The target of these demonstrations was the construction industry, because any-one who marvels at America's skyscraper chase to the sky must have noticed the strongly white cast of the construction workers on the job.

Would anyone seriously submit that this is mere coincidence? Abundant evidence exists of systematic exclusion of black peo-ple from these high-placed, high-paying jobs. Who is primarily responsible? Some people suggest that American craft unions, particularly the construction trade unions, harbor large numbers of racists within their ranks and that they are responsible.

In any event, these protests produced desired shutdowns and tie-ups and undesired counterdemonstrations. There were fresh attempts at negotiation. However, though the source of this problem may well be the construction industry, there is at least one other major institutional villain as well. Enforceable statutes make it *government's* legal duty to eliminate racial discrimination in the construction industry. Government's trump over con-tractors lies in awarding fat contracts for erection of state build-ings or for state-funded construction. The money involved is ample, so that if the right levers are pulled, the right strings jiggle.

Recently, a committee was formed to examine the New York state government's performance in this area. Consisting of one lawyer (the unsuccessful Democratic candidate for New York attorney general in 1970, Adam Walinsky) and several law and political science graduate students, this group was known as the Committee for Efficiency in Government (CEG). It issued a report in the spring of 1970 on "official lawlessness in New York State" which zeroed in on government complicity in maintaining heavy discrimination against black Americans, but particularly black New Yorkers.

There are several New York state agencies that can twist the proper arms, and many laws that could be used to apply effective pressure. The germane agencies include the State Division of Human Rights; the Department of Law under the attorney general; the Department of Labor; the Industrial Commissioner; and the Office of General Services.

As for legal weapons, CEG noted that (1) the "State can void any construction contract where discriminatory practices are found"; and (2) "the hiring process must give preference to New York State citizens, and a contract must be voided for failure to give such preference." This last provision, I might add, is to help remove unemployed people from the New York welfare dole. Further, (3) "all construction companies trading with the State of New York are required to keep an accurate accounting of the names of their employees, noting particularly whether or not they are citizens of the state." The industrial commissioner is responsible for presenting to the agency that contracted for the work evidence of noncompliance with the "citizens" provision. The agency is then supposed to force the company to obey the fair-hiring provisions.

Now for the facts found by the CEG:

(1) Poverty among black families in New York City increased by a whopping 46 percent in the eight years between 1960 and 1968.

(2) The construction industry is the only goods-producing

industry in New York that increased its number of jobs from 1955 to 1965. Furthermore, construction work doesn't require a high school diploma, so that blacks who fail to achieve one are not formally disqualified, as they are in so many other industries.

(3) Although the black population of New York City is significant, the percentage of blacks working in the construction industry in 1967 was only 2 percent.

(4) On construction of the South Mall state government project in Albany, in the late sixties, the percentage of blacks on construction work was also "on the border of 2 percent. . . ."

(5) "The critical fact of construction employment in New York is that a great proportion of it is carried out by craftsmen brought in from other states, and even from Canada." For instance, CEG estimated that 15 percent of new construction jobs in the Buffalo area were filled by Canadians. It might be noted that about 20 percent of the population of Buffalo is black. The Canadian-wetback situation also typifies contracts signed by New York State for work on the Albany Mall and the statewide expansion of the State University of New York (SUNY) system.

(6) There would seem to be a drastic discrepancy between the laws of the State of New York and hiring practices in constructing state projects.

What has the State of New York done to help ease this intolerable and illegal situation? Nothing to very little. Official dawdling has been a key factor in helping the construction industry constrict black opportunity.

In 1965, the State Division of Human Rights was empowered to initiate complaints of racial discrimination based on facts established by its own investigation. From 1965 to 1970, the State Division of Human Rights (SDHR) managed to institute one study on its own and has initiated no complaint. In response to a flood of complaints, it has refused to hold hearings in 92 percent of cases related to the construction industry. Considering the tiny percentage of blacks employed in the industry, and the large number of Canadians earning construction paychecks, it seems strange that the agency didn't believe the complaints warranted a hearing.

What about the State Department of Labor and the industrial commissioner? CEG feels that those responsible forces were even "less active in enforcing the law than is the SDHR." The industrial commissioner is directed by law to deregister any apprenticeship program when "objective evidence" is found that certain standards for admission to apprenticeship are not maintained. Yet despite the fact that the attorney general's office of the State of New York has successfully initiated complaints against discriminatory apprenticeship programs over the last few years, "no apprenticeship program has ever been deregistered by the industrial commissioner." Findings by the attorney general are apparently not "objective evidence" enough for the commissioner's office. Does this constitute a willful or malicious failure to act, contrary to law? If not, what is?

CEG has cause to be glum.

> The consistent pattern we found: nonenforcement of state laws, disregard of powerful weapons to eliminate discrimination and half-hearted efforts in areas of little importance, these patterns lead us to conclude that not only are the highest officers of the state administration aware of the discrimination against nonwhites, but that those men have made it a conscious and deliberate policy to condone and even support its continuation.[4]

If CEG is correct, there is a famine of law and order in the administration of the antidiscrimination codes of New York State, one that has reduced them to a skeleton of the body of law they were designed to be.

ENTER MR. PERSECUTING ATTORNEY

As serious as the maladministration of public welfare and antidiscrimination laws can be, there is another type that is much worse, though perhaps more rare, because the consequences can be lethal. Lethal, because the administrator in this instance is the public prosecutor: the district attorney, the United States attorney, or whatever his title may be. Can it be that the man responsible for activating the criminal process against another human being may himself criminally violate other laws he has vowed to obey? So much for rhetorical questions.

One highly questionable procedure has become an integral part of the job of prosecutor which makes it, despite a lack of foundation in American jurisprudence, part of our operating system of justice. According to all authoritative sources, the American legal system considers the prosecuting attorney an officer of the court. He is required to remain as objective as possbile; his sworn duty is to seek justice, not conviction. Another way to put this is to say that the theoretical role of the prosecutor is to prosecute, not persecute, to protect the innocent as well as to prosecute the guilty. As the Supreme Court of the United States said with its occasional literary flair:

> The United States Attorney is a representative not of an ordinary party to a controversy, but of a sovereignty whose obligation to govern impartially is as compelling as its obligation to govern at all; and whose interest, therefore, in a criminal prosecution is not that it shall win a case, but that justice shall be done. . . . It is as much his duty to refrain from improper methods calculated to produce a wrongful conviction as it is to use every legitimate means to bring about a just one.[5]

That is "the system" as it is supposed to be, "the system" as our scrolls, textbooks, and fairytales would have us believe it actually works. But the facts indicate the cruel contrary, and lawyers, as well as those in professional relationship to the criminal enforcement process (including criminals), know that it is not that way at all. This clear role mandate is the exception that proves the rule to the contrary. "Realists" and pragmatists scoff at the general ideals stated above, saying that they are, of course, impractical. But even the most practical skeptics would not advocate that a prosecuting attorney be free to lie or intimidate criminal suspects, even if they know that this is the way it happens all too often.

Perhaps the most widely condoned persecutorial practice in our functioning system is that of plea bargaining. Since prosecutors are interested in "expediting" the criminal process, they desire a conviction as cheaply as possible in terms of time spent getting it. Frequently, a prosecutor feels he has sufficient evidence to convict a man on a higher charge. If the suspect is pleading not guilty, the prosecutor will tell him to plead guilty to a lesser charge, and the higher charge will be dropped. Self-styled pragmatists think this practice is necessary oil to a system creaking under an intolerably heavy load.

> The Payne case was only one of 500 indictments on Judge Richard Fitzgerald's docket last year; it would have taken him four years to try them all. So 85 to 90 percent of them ended in plea bargaining—that backstairs haggling process by which pleas of guilty are bartered for reduced charges or shorter sentences or probation. "Plea bargaining used to be a nasty word," says Fitzgerald; only lately have the bar and the courts begun to call it out of the closet and recognize it as not just a reality but a necessity of the system. "We're becoming a little more sophisticated about it. We're saying 'You're doing it, we know you're doing it and you have to do it; this is the way it has to be done.' " [6]

It has to be done because "the system" is too cheap to buy a numerically adequate and professionally competent judiciary. And even though plea bargaining expedites the criminal process, it also facilitates far more injustice than would be the case if such "haggling" were not going on in the closet. Plea bargaining is simply an arrogant and callous disregard of what the prosecutor's role is supposed to be. And it has inherent dangers as well.

One of them leads directly to a pernicious type of prosecutorial lawlessness. For permitting (or encouraging) prosecutors to bargain with a suspect over his life and liberty gives the prosecutor latitude to fudge a bit.

For example, some DA's have been known to "overcharge," that is, pin a charge they are unsure of establishing on a suspect. In order to avoid trial on the lesser, but more "convictable," charge, he will then bargain with the suspect to plead guilty on that lesser charge. In return for the guilty plea, he promises to drop the overcharge. Some bargain.

Frequently the defendant is poor or ignorant of the situation, or may have a young and inexperienced criminal lawyer or over-loaded Public Defender, and the "deal" looks fair enough. But this does not prove the suspect was guilty of either charge; he simply opted for an "easier" way out of a dilemma illegally created by the prosecutor. If we bring this out of the closet, we will be exposing the deceit of some DA's, which isn't a bad idea. For such betrayal of his oath to seek justice instead of convictions is an action well beyond the demands of the system he is pledged to uphold.

Occasionally, prosecutors completely lose their objectivity and their cool, and strive to put someone behind bars at all costs, not to expedite under the system, but to get that individual. Whatever the reason—hatred, overambitiousness, or fear of admitting error (or a combination of all three)—prosecutors lie, cheat, scheme, and struggle to convict a man on the basis of evidence they know is unworthy, or by concealing evidence they know works to the advantage of the defense.

Two recent Supreme Court cases provide an illustration of each. In *Miller v. Pate,* decided in 1969,[7] the facts, as found by the Supreme Court of the United States, were as follows:

A particularly brutal sex crime had been committed in Illinois, in which an eight-year-old girl was raped and slain. The community howled for blood. They got it in the form of a major item of evidence, a pair of men's undershorts found about a mile away from the site of the crime. The shorts were drenched in blood. Their owner was the man on trial.

Throughout the trial, the prosecuting attorney constantly referred to these "bloody" and "bloodstained" shorts. It was established by an expert that the defendant's blood type was O. The prosecutor made much of this fact because the blood on the the defendant's shorts, according to the prosecuting attorney, was the blood of the little girl. This theme was hammered home again and again. Not surprisingly, the defendant was convicted of murder.

Years later, the defendant managed to win a hearing on a writ of *habeas corpus* in a Federal District Court. At that proceeding, some rather interesting expert testimony came to pass. Another chemist, after microanalyzing the shorts, found that the notorious underwear had no blood on them after all. Those spots were, as a matter of fact, *paint*. The microanalyst found "no traces of human blood" on the "bloody" shorts. This could not have been a total revelation to Mr. Prosecuting Attorney. Since the police had previously prepared a memorandum for him attempting to explain "how this exhibit contains all the paint on it," he must have had knowledge of this fact at the trial itself.

The only counterargument advanced by the state, in light of the new testimony, was that the jury knew that there was paint on the shorts. But the Supreme Court repeated the statements of the prosecutor at trial, none of which mentioned paint and all of which made the point-blank assertion that the shorts were bloody. The Supreme Court concluded that "the record of the petitioner's trial reflects the prosecution's consistent and repeated misrepresentation that People's Exhibit 3 was, indeed, 'a garment heavily stained with blood!' "

The Court went on to say, "The prosecution's whole theory with respect to the exhibit depended on those misrepresentations." The Court concluded, "The prosecutor deliberately misrepresented the truth." In other words, he was a liar.

He might also be considered guilty of a number of other things the Court left unmentioned. A prosecutor who deliberately conceals evidence in the face of the court could be held responsible for criminal libel, abuse of the criminal process, contempt of court, and, perhaps, kidnaping. After all, such license with the truth could mean that it was a prosecutor's intent to deprive a defendant of his freedom, if not his life, for a period of years with no legitimate grounds. That could fit some definitions of kidnaping.

Also, in 1967, the Court found substantial evidence of similar prosecutorial misconduct, this time in the state of Maryland.[8] Once again, it was a sex crime, an alleged rape of a sixteen-year-old white girl by three black men. The defendants were convicted. There was a posttrial reexamination of the evidence occasioned by the alleged "suppression of evidence" by a prosecutor—evidence, as the Supreme Court found, that would have been vital to the defense's case.

In rape cases, the customary sexual behavior of the complaining female is at issue, particularly when the defense maintains she consented to the intercourse. What is involved is her credibility. Was she raped? Did she consent? Did she encourage the man? Her previous behavior, her reputation, her statements and actions, or any evidence relevant to her believability, is particularly relevant. In the South, in border states—frankly, in most places in America—white males (including officials) are peculiarly unable to believe that a white girl would consent to sexual relations with a black man, much less a gang of black men. In the Maryland case, there was weighty evidence available to the prosecutor that could have led him to the conclusion that the complaining witness was a nymphomaniac.

For example, subsequent to the alleged rape incident, but before the trial, the girl complained of another ravage by two other men. Shortly thereafter, she attempted suicide, whereupon she was shipped to a mental institution. While there, she told police she had had previous intercourse with one of the two men involved in the second "rape," as well as with numerous other men. This information, known to the prosecutor, was never relayed to the defense.

Moreover, some statements by the girl in the police report about the main rape incident were inconsistent. She said one thing to the police at the time, and narrated quite another story at the trial. Two key inconsistencies related to (1) whether she had had sexual relations in the car with her boyfriend before the three "rapists" arrived and (2) whether two or three of the interlopers had "raped" her.

Surely all of this was pertinent for the jury to consider in a case where the credibility of the complainant was such an important facet. Yet none of the above evidence was made available to the defense, and thus not to the jury either. It was suppressed. Due to this suppression, the Supreme Court of the United States reversed the conviction. Justice Abe Fortas, in the concurring opinion, put it this way:

> I do not agree that the State may be excused from its duty to disclose material facts known to it prior to trial solely because of a conclusion that they would not be admissible at trial. The state's obligation is not to convict, but to see that, so far as possible, truth emerges. . . .
>
> This is not to say that convictions ought to be reversed on the ground that information . . . without importance to the defense for purposes of the preparation of the case or for trial was not disclosed to defense counsel. . . . But this is not the case. . . . The information was specific, factual and concrete . . . the information withheld was directly related to that defense.[9]

Justice Fortas went on to say that the prosecutor had deprived the defendant of his right to a fair trial under the Fourteenth Amendment. If done with intent, it would be a violation of the Civil Rights Act, a federal crime.

In the Maryland case, a prosecutorial intention to deceive was not as clear as it was in the Painted Shorts Caper. But there is sufficient room to suspect that the Maryland district attorney's actions were meant to hide this evidence because he personally wanted the jury to believe these three men raped that one girl. Whether he believed it himself is unimportant. If he didn't, then of course he misused his position intentionally to force innocent men into jail, and is therefore guilty of the same malice as was the prosecutor in the Illinois case. If he believed the girl, but felt this new evidence might confuse the jury and lead to their erroneously disbelieving her, and he intentionally suppressed the evidence for the the sake of justice, he is still guilty of intentionally violating his role as a court officer.

Good intentions make not one shred of difference; such acts can amount to official anarchy as practiced in the United States by some prosecuting attorneys. There are too many convictions in America reversed by higher courts for illegal suppression of evidence by a state or federal attorney. No serious sanctions against the prosecutor, much less an investigation into his intent, follow.

Let me relate two more unusual types of alleged persecutorial malconduct, just to complete my brief on the many faces of prosecutorial anarchy.

The first has to do with a band of about 180 black nationalists who were holding a convention in a small church in Detroit early in 1969. A disturbance outside the church between several black men and a police patrol resulted in the killing of one of the policemen and the wounding of the other. The survivor radioed for help, and a small army of policemen landed shortly thereafter. Digging in, they raked the church with rifle fire, pumping pounds of bullets into the chapel.

After the barrage, they stormed the church and arrested everyone in sight. This large group of men and women was jailed and kept incommunicado for some six hours before a black judge, George Crockett, finally arrived at the station. He had been awakened and informed of the situation at 5 A.M. by two black leaders in the Detroit area who had gotten wind of the situation, and wanted a little overdue process.

Judge Crockett convened his court to hear the charges against all these people. None were lodged against most of them. Therefore, the judge released them, one by one. After some thirty-nine of them had been freed, the Wayne County prosecutor arrived and countermanded the court order to bring the other prisoners forward. The judge demanded that the prosecutor refrain from interfering with the *habeas corpus* proceedings, but the prosecutor pressed on. A stalemate ensued and the court was adjourned.

Afterward, the prosecutor agreed that some 130 more of the arrestees should be released. However, another series of disagreements arose between judge and prosecutor, and the prosecutor refused on several occasions to honor the court with any sound reason why he should not be held in contempt. The issue was never resolved because Judge Crockett refused to cite the DA. He felt the prosecutor's apparent bias had brought him (Judge Crockett) into an unresolvable conflict of interest with his own impartiality. But the fact remained that the prosecutor had sided with the police, flouting judicial commands in violation of his oath of office. The prosecutor had insisted on keeping over one hundred people in jail though there was no evidence against the vast majority of them. It was, as the judge later told me, a "prosecutorial dragnet."

The second type involves a variation of "overcharging," one where a prosecutor wants more than legal chips for plea bargaining. An excellent illustration surfaced only recently when a Maryland prosecutor accused one of his colleagues of "fabricating" a false arson complaint against H. Rap Brown. Why might a state prosecutor do something like that? According to Richard Kinlein, the state's prosecutor in Howard County, Maryland, his colleague in Dorchester County, William Yates, told him privately that he had drummed up this unsupportable charge against Brown so the FBI could be brought into the case.

The state's main grudge against Brown was for allegedly inciting a riot in Cambridge, Maryland, a charge which is simply a misdemeanor in Maryland. Prosecutor Yates might have figured that Brown would duck Maryland's quest for justice, and he could have wanted Brown in hotter water than he would be for sidestepping a minor Maryland trial. If someone neglects to appear for a state felony trial, he commits a federal crime (unlawful interstate flight) and becomes fair game for the FBI. Kinlein asserted that Yates admitted he had no evidence of any acts of arson by Brown. That is why, in Kinlein's view, the indictment was "phony" and a "perversion of justice." [10]

Given the contemporary American prosecutorial system that commends the practicality of tampering with charges, adding a felony count to an indictment in order to ensure some future federal help in the case shouldn't alarm many people. A prosecutor might do this to ensure that justice, as he sees it, is done. But falsification of charges, if true, no matter how just the desired end, is still a maliciously lawless act. Charges of such should be thoroughly investigated. But they aren't. They are scoffed at— and usually forgotten. Prosecutors seem to have an aversion to prosecuting fellow prosecutors. Is it any wonder?

WHEN BLACK ISN'T DUTIFUL

More frightening, some bureaucratic outlaws take fierce pride in their handiwork. In fact, some bureaucratic tyranny is accompanied by official boasting and public praise. Administrative lawlessness has been known to perform to an acclaim that smacks ominously of a populace clapping itself into an invisible prison.

The case of Angela Davis versus the Board of Regents of the University of California is a prime example. Many of Miss Davis' credentials are popularly known because of her well-reported entanglements with the law over the 1970 Marin County Courthouse shootout. But some are important enough to bear repeating here to demonstrate what a clear-cut case of grandstanding official anarchy looks like.

UCLA hired Angela Davis to teach philosophy. At that time, she was a fairly well known black militant in the Southern California area. An honors student at Brandeis during her undergraduate career, she had advanced to study at the Sorbonne and subsequently became a favorite of the past master mentor of modern American radicals, Herbert Marcuse. Under Marcuse's tutelage at the University of California at San Diego, she earned her master's degree in philosophy.

In those golden days of yore, when prestigious American universities panted for professionally trained black instructors to make token appearances on their campuses, Angela Davis was breakfast at Tiffany's. But there was a fly in the academic ointment. Angela, alas, was a Communist—an out-and-out, bona fide, honest-to-goodness, card-carrying Commie; not a pinko, mind you, a brilliant red. Needless to say, it didn't take long before that colorful fact made its public debut. There was a Communist on the UCLA faculty, and her name was Angela Davis.

Naturally, this sort of disclosure attracted political notice. A clamor arose. Its purpose? To rid UCLA of all Communists. This meant that some people wanted Angela exorcised. They wanted her out anyway, but being a Communist made her a pariah to even more people, including "liberals" who know when they are licked.

The University of California system has long been rated at the top of the American college world. One reason for its (past?) preeminence has been its relative immunity from political pressures, at least since the early fifties. Part of this immunity was due to a golden rule, the Board of Regents' own standing order No. 102.1: "No political test shall ever be considered in the appointment and promotion of any faculty member. . . ." In other words, "Thou shalt not rid UCLA of faculty members you dislike politically."

Meanwhile, back at the Westwood campus, Angela Davis was under close scrutiny. Her classes were heavily monitored, tape recorders, vigilantes, the gamut. She knew that one false move and she would be O-U-T. But she was good. Very good. "Articulate," said some. "Open-minded and fair," said others. Her credentials were, as indicated, impeccable. But this did not stop the Reaganized Board of Regents of the University of California. They ousted her outright. On what ground? Because she was an avowed member of the Communist Party, U.S.A. Consorting with such a treacherous organization meant to the Board of Regents that she was *ipso facto* treacherous. So they said publicly and proudly that she must go, and their decision was met with substantial public approval.

But there was that pesky rule on their own books that said that no one could be discharged because of their political beliefs, wasn't there? Yes. Then how could the Board of Regents act against the law? And what about freedom of speech? And academic freedom?

With public apathy ringing in her ears, Miss Davis was forced to take the matter to court, where the trial judge agreed with her. It was a clear case of official anarchy. Judge Jerry Pacht, of the Superior Court of California, reversed the Board of Regents because they had violated the law and discharged this faculty member only because of her political affiliation. He observed that in so doing the Regents had constituted themselves as a "political elite empowered to decide whose views were dangerous or palatable." The judge noted that by definition such an elite is "anathema to the concept of a free university and a free people."

> The court believes it would be unlawful and dangerous to allow the Regents to dip political litmus paper into the volatile cauldron of political controversy in order to determine the academic qualifications of faculty members.[11]

So Angela won—that time. But only because the Regents were so arrogant and forthright in their lawlessness. The bulk of the public enjoyed it. Only a court insisted on adherence to the law. However, the Regents managed to give her the fire next time, when they played a more sophisticated game. Despite their open breach of the law the first time, nothing happened to them personally. Miss Davis, on the other hand, had to cover some heavy legal expenses. But that was small change compared to another, similar, case.

Once upon a time there was a well known black fighter by the name of Muhammad Ali. He was the undisputed heavy-weight champion of the world, and could and did lick every man in the house.

Ali liked to hear himself talk and many wayward words flowed from his Louisville Lip. Some of his prose made droves of people angry. For instance, Ali charged that America was a racist society, and that the Vietnam War was a result of American imperialist aggression. He also said that no black man should allow himself to be sucked into the mess in Vietnam, because the real fight for freedom was in America—by black men, for their own liberty.

All of this was bad enough, but Ali went further. He acted. Or rather, he failed to act when it was his duty to act. He failed to step forward at his draft induction. He refused to serve in the armed forces of the United States. The reason he gave for refusing to fight a war was that all war was against his religious belief as a Black Muslim minister. According to the tenets of that religion, all war is immoral.

In any event, the federal government found his plea of conscientious objection incredible and brought him to trial. The trial was a criminal trial, and the Texas jury of his peers decided that he was guilty as charged. Ali's attorneys filed for appeal.

Muhammad Ali was now a convict. He was free on bail, but he had been convicted of a federal felony. Several state boxing commissions justified revoking his license to box in their states on these shaky grounds. There was precedent, of course, for refusing to allow a boxer who was a criminal to fight. Certain circumstances in the Ali case made it quite different. One major one was that he was still appealing his conviction on a question of law. In other words, until the appellate courts of the United States government had decided either against him or not to hear his appeal, it was still unsettled whether Ali was a criminal.

Yet the New York State Boxing Commission countermanded its own favorable precedent (allowing men with criminal records to box in New York) and denied Ali his livelihood. In fact, as the NAACP pointed out in its brief for Muhammad Ali, the New York State Athletic Commission had a tradition of granting licenses to convicts—even for military offenses. In 1970, over ninety convicts with no appeals pending were allowed to fight in New York.

Small wonder, then, that a Federal District Court overruled these administrators on the Ali case. But it took three years off a champion's fighting life. The court stated that the action of refusing to grant Muhammad Ali a license was "arbitrary and unreasonable." [12] There was obvious discrimination against Ali as a man, not as a convict, and this was therefore "unequal protection of the law" by a state government agency.

Furthermore, to the degree that this bureaucratic action was unlikely to be a mistake, one could infer willingness and intent on their part. They probably knew their action would cause him grievous personal and financial injury. And after all, why should a man who refuses to fight for his country benefit financially from fighting in this country? Such sentiments are common in the land of the free.

But the New York commissioners were government officials. If they acted out their personal dislike for that man or his political or religious beliefs, then they acted illegally and unlawfully deprived him of lots of bread and more than a few pats of butter. The courts made it clear that they had arbitrarily discriminated against Ali. Still, nothing was ever done to these commissioners, despite the fact that a good case could be made that they cost Ali millions of dollars by their illegal action.

WELL, SHUT MY MOUTH

Another classic incident of widely applauded bureaucratic lawlessness involved the Selective Service System. As everyone knows, the SSS was run by a vintage public servant named Lewis Hershey, who was by trade a retired field marshal. Hershey, who shepherded Selective Service from the onset of World War Two, became as much a personification of the draft as J. Edgar Hoover has been a personification of the G-man.

Prior to the Vietnam War, Hershey was a laconic man, an apolitical man. Or so Americans thought. After all, his job was simple enough: the Army needed to conscript men, and he was to expedite their transformation from Mister to Private Jones. But the Vietnam War produced a cloud of flak from the cannon fodder itself. Many men did not want to go, and many didn't want others to go either.

This view was a bone that stuck in Hershey's craw. After all, to the degree that these recalcitrant men might be successful in arguing their position against serving in Vietnam, they would interfere with General Hershey's prime function, and nothing rankles administrators more than being told they and their work are immoral and should go into receivership. Since the courts were being slow to convict draft resisters and accomplices before the fact, Hershey got worried. So he acted: he wrote a letter, which he was not reluctant to defend in public.

This epic epistle was greeted warmly by Selective Service boards all over America. Let it be clear, though, that it was not an order. What the general did was to encourage the bored members to reclassify some of their registrants as 1-A. Who was to be reclassified? Well, the majority of them were probably students. For what reason were they to be reclassified? There had been pockets of protest against the Vietnam War, and one then current method of displaying student scorn for that war was to return one's draft card to the authorities, including the draft board, or to reissue it as ashes. Draft boards receiving ashes usually jumped to the conclusion that they were the remains of the sender's draft card. It was not too gauche an inference to make.

One young man, Earl Gutknecht, exercised greater restraint in his expression of symbolic contempt. He simply tossed his draft credentials at the feet of a United States marshal at a rally. Gutknecht was already 1-A, though, and was appealing his status as a conscientious objector. His appeal was made moot by a hasty decision of his draft board to induct him within five days. He refused to be inducted, was tried and convicted. His board didn't even give him the full appeal time on the C.O. application.

This really upset the Supreme Court of the United States, which once again reversed the action of an unruly bureaucracy. Justice William O. Douglas noted that there "is no suggestion in the current draft law that the Selective Service has freewheeling authority to ride herd on the registrants, using immediate induction as a disciplinary or vindictive measure," [13] which was exactly what was being done to Gutknecht and many others. Some draft boards were construing participation in antiwar demonstrations as "delinquency" and were withdrawing deferments on that basis. The Army was being used as a penal institution for those who opposed the Vietnam War.

Draft boards continued to be enormously persistent in trying to open the Army to students to help them keep their mouths closed. On some occasions, boards defied court orders to the contrary. One such case occurred in New York, where the draft board reclassified a student—they withdrew his student deferment—because, as they said initially, his grades were too low. The judge reviewing the board's action commented that it was both "high-handed" and "erroneous," [14] and ordered the board to drop the induction order. The board did so.

Unwilling to give up, however, they did something else. They rescanned their records and found some justification for reclassifying him one year retroactively, making the student re-eligible for the draft. He returned to court to enlist the aid of the judge again. The judge was forced to conclude that the retroactive reclassification was "wholly unauthorized either by statute or regulation." The judge believed the board was being vengeful and said so. He thought the board was trying to "accelerate petitioner's eventual induction without due process, as punishment for his temerity in resorting to the courts for vindication and protection of his legal rights." The judge, an honorable man, went on to call the board's action "lawless."

The actions of such boards were understandable in light of the attitudes of many associated with the Selective Service System. General Hershey and many of his subordinates felt that an Army stint was just punishment for young men with insufficient patriotism. But the laws that limit the SSS do not equate induction into the Army with a term in a penitentiary.

Civil servants, including those who serve on draft boards, are obliged to run their offices equitably and to refrain from allowing their politics and those of their clients to influence their job. The Selective Service System from Hershey on down was interfering lawlessly and arrogantly in the American political process by trying to muzzle lawful dissent against a particular policy college students happened to find especially repugnant. If the arson of draft cards or harassment of military recruitment was illegal, then this was a matter for the Department of Justice and the federal courts to decide.

This usurpation of power was a purely arbitrary act to penalize American citizens, and was completely above and beyond the call of the law. All that happened to Hershey was that he was eventually promoted (kicked upstairs). The Regents who shot down Angela and the boxing commissioners who robbed Muhammad Ali of those prime years suffer nothing but a few harsh words from a judge. In these cases, official lawlessness brought public esteem and official rewards. Government, as a faction, protects its own.

The spread of administrative lawlessness is, of course, commensurate with the sprawl of public bureaucracy throughout our society. It can be found in all bureaus, throughout all levels of government. I've mentioned some of the more arcane and some of the more blatant; I've portrayed some of the cruder, and some of the more polished. I've failed to spend time on some of the more ludicrous, like post office snooping into our mails.[15]

I've not dwelt on teacher's strikes, police sick-ins ("blue flu"), or postal shutdowns, even though probably more government workers take part in this kind of administrative lawlessness than all the others combined. I've not gone into the crisis of government electronic surveillance and big-brother-is-watching-you-ism. As the reader might know, the Nixon administration is pushing for externally unchecked bureaucratic power to wiretap, bug, and bother as it sees fit in certain types of cases (so they say). Meanwhile, a sticky network of illegal wiretapping and eavesdropping already exists, and threatens to grow.

In other words, I've been arbitrarily selective. But that's what is most alarming. By picking and choosing almost at random among the illustrations of administrative anarchy in modern America, a frightening picture emerges. It's like a middle-aged Dorian Gray. The portrait is already grotesque enough, but it has years to deteriorate.

POGONOGO would paint a totally different canvas.

6

Judicial
Anarchy

You be the judge.
   —*Old American saying*

Heah come de judge.
   —*New American saying*

Lawyers don't fare particularly well in the eternal competition for prestige in America. This legal status hiatus exists perhaps because lawyers are, in some ways, like call girls. They sell their ample talents—in this case legal training—for a price. Thereafter, their affections flow generously. That is the nature of their job. They are inclined to favor clients' needs. And, as advocates, since they must speak for a client, they must present their client's view as forcefully, eloquently, and passionately as the client would, could he.

But despite the skill, training, and talent poured into the practice of law, pity the poor lawyer. The practice of law still elicits abundant scorn from the average man. In polls that seek to establish a ladder of occupational prestige, for instance, lawyers always trail physicians, and they usually lag behind professors as well. But though doctors may be called "sawbones," that does not connote the same degree of disgust as vituperations reserved for lawyers. When someone calls a lawyer "shyster," everyone nods and knows. Such is the cross that a mercenary advocate of causes must bear.

Judges, on the other hand, are widely admired. Comparing stereotypes of the judge and the lawyer is a study in extremes. This is a bit surprising, since nearly all American judges were practicing lawyers before being appointed or elected to the bench. The fact remains that being a judge is highly prestigious, despite his training and experience as a considerably less admirable attorney.

The "typical" judge is thought to be distinguished-looking, silver-maned, calm, fatherly, and wise. He is considered aloof but compassionate. He is believed to be judicious in manner and just in decision. And so it has gone for eons in America, from Judge Hardy to Kenesaw Mountain Landis, because Americans, for the most part, have bought the judicial image as it is projected in professional role expectations for judges. Judges have been considered to do and be that which they are professionally expected to do and be. While the skinning of lawyers is endemic in movies and on TV, the media have been soft on judges. It is extraordinary to see a judge misbehave in *any* visual medium; it would be like seeing Granny commit sodomy.

The two most fundamental expectations for our judges are impartiality and independence. Impartiality, in our system, means that every judge is supposed to be bound by case precedent. That is, judges are compelled to defer to general principles of law laid down by higher courts in their own jurisdiction. Even when their own personal viewpoint might conflict with what that law reads, they are supposed to follow the law, and keep their own personal feelings about the parties or the issues to themselves.

For instance, in a nerve-gas-dumping case in Florida in 1969, the courts were the final hurdle for the Army. The judge, in refusing to enjoin the Army from sinking poison gas into the Atlantic, made a point of saying that she disagreed with the Army, but that it was within the Army's legal discretion to make the decision. This is what is legally meant by impartiality, or objectivity. It is everyone's freedom from a judge's internal hangups.

Independence, on the other hand, involves an external objectivity. In other words, to be impartial, a judge must brace himself against his own prejudices. To be independent, he must fortify himself against pressures from outside sources, particularly his fellows in government.

In America, the judiciary is an indivisible branch of government, and its job is to arbitrate conflicts between parties. Since government often becomes embroiled in legal disputes (every criminal case involves the state), however, judges find themselves in the ironic position of being part of government, but being charged with the responsibility to keep their minds free from assuming that government is correct, good, or just.

CLAY FEET AND CLAY PIGEONS

So much for ideas and stereotypes. Judges, like other American government idols, have come to be seen lately as having feet of clay. Shorn of the protection of illusion, they have become attractive political game. But though open season has been declared on judges only recently, there was preparation for it in the past.

Strangely enough, the first attacks on the accuracy of the role concepts of judicial impartiality and judicial objectivity were mounted by judges and philosophers of jurisprudence. Maybe that's not too strange—after all, they ought to know. A movement in law school circles known as "legal realism" was the beginning. Legal realists scoffed at the traditional line that judges simply interpreted the law, and did not make it. They said that judges, like all men, injected their own prejudices into their decisions. This was the initial sortie into the judicial inner sanctum.

As the years rolled by, other academic disciplines began sniping at the courts (or, I should say, tried to shoot holes into the court mythology). In American sociology, it was the "sociology of law" faction, and in American political science in the 1960's it was the "judicial behaviorists." By the late sixties, the hunt peaked with squads of social scientists repeatedly demonstrating the legal realists' opinion that judges' decisions were frequently, if not usually, based on their own personal values, ideology, philosophy, and attitudes.

Their studies also indicated that many other extralegal factors, such as judges' background, experiences, training, and political party affiliation, were quite closely related to differences in the ways judges decided cases. As so often happens, academic and juristic attacks laid the foundation for political ones that were to come and which remain, for better or for worse, a popular national pastime.

Of course, there has been *political* poaching on the American judiciary dating from the first time American courts tried to flex their puny muscles. Thomas Jefferson frothed and fulminated against the federal judiciary for its administration of the Alien and Sedition Acts at the turn of the nineteenth century. And President John Adams, recognizing some potential political leverage in the courts, made sure one of his own, John Marshall, occupied the head stewardship of the Supreme Court for a long lifetime stay. Then there was the dreadful Scott decision, and some time later, the trouble American courts caused while resisting pressures for social reform legislation around the turn of our century.

In the nineteen thirties, the "nine old men" and the "court-packing scheme" were important phrases in FDR's raids against a fuddy-duddy Supreme Court. At that time, the "liberals" were after the Court's blood. Then, when the Warren Court made its Kabuki-like entrance into the legal field of racial segregation and manifested its concern about individual rights against the police power, the "conservatives" loaded their weapons.

The Supreme Court is not the only target; lower court judges, too, are drawing increasing fire. At the local level, for instance, the San Diego police fraternal order tried to punish judges it believed to be coddling criminals. They developed a plan to grade judicial sentencing behavior, and to publicize the permissive tendencies of those judges who were loosing waves of bloodthirsty villains on a helpless public. In California, you see, judges are elected. The very threat of such publicity, particularly in a conservative area like San Diego, could force judges to decide other than they might without such pressure.

The left wing has also been actively anticourt lately, at all levels. For new lefters have witnessed a series of events in the past decade that have convinced them, too, that judges have been much less objective and impartial than they were supposed to be. Much is still being said and written about this, with the usual leftist zeal, and has resulted in some novel antijudicial tactics.

For example, some of the more radical of the new left have decided to repudiate the judicial system at the outset of every trial. In their view, no judge can be impartial toward them or remain independent. Without these prerequisites for judiciousness, they believe there can be no real court. Court disrupters do not feel their antics are contempt of court, but simply contempt for the judge's contempt of his own judicial role.

This explains the spirited spectaculars staged in some courtrooms lately. Is the right right? Is the left right? When does a judge become worthy of political pressures or of disrespect, or rate impeachment or indictment?

The big problem is how to draw a line between legitimate discretion, abuse of it, and intentional disdain of the judicial requirement of impartiality for some supralegal reason. Howard James, in his book *Crisis in the Courts*,[1] developed an elegant eleven-part classification of judicial incompetence: (1) hacks, (2) retirees, (3) failures, (4) the inattentive, (5) misfits, (6) the informal, (7) the incapacitated, (8) the inexperienced, (9) the lazy, (10) the weak, and (11) the prejudiced.

Only two of them are directly relevant to judicial anarchy, i.e., incompetents 5 and 11. For although the others are bad enough, in their own way, they lack the strength and will to intentionally violate the law that characterize "judicial lawlessness." For instance, James sees the misfits as being abnormally "abrasive" and "short-tempered"—individuals who "come to court with their minds made up."[2] The prejudiced are similar to the misfits; they refuse to shed their own biases, and intentionally mete out strict judgments to those in their disfavor. James gives us an example of "old-fashioned prejudice": "When I asked a

Miami, Fla., judge why he gave a surprisingly severe sentence to a Spanish-speaking youth, he explained that the boy was of a migrant family." [3]

Not all intentional ignoring of established law is judicial lawlessness. For instance, the Supreme Court decision in *Brown v. Board of Education* reversed a precedent, an action well within the Supreme Court's prerogative.[4] In an important sense it was a policy decision, not aimed at any specific persons. No one suggests that in not following the law, the justices exercised personal pique at some individual school superintendent. Furthermore, reversal of prior decisions by a high court is allowable under the common-law system, though it is rarely done. The idea of official anarchy, or judicial anarchy, does not apply to a decision or a pattern of precedent-reversal decisions by the Supreme Court. One may disagree with the nature and basis of a decision of the Supreme Court, but one cannot press to indict them for a crime merely because one doesn't like the way the decision went or because a justice voted to overrule a precedent.

Most judges open to anarchy charges sit at the trial level, for they deal directly with the parties, not just with silk-stockinged attorneys making abstract arguments. Furthermore, whereas appellate judges—specifically those at the highest level—are permitted to reverse relevant precedents, trial judges are not. The trial judge must follow precedent, no matter what his attitudes, and no matter what the situation may be. His role in this is clear.

The two major types of American judicial lawlessness occur when a judge (1) flagrantly violates his oath to stay within the law, or (2) wages a personal vendetta against some poor soul, individually or as a representative of a group. The crucial element is the *mens rea*, that is, whether the judge intends to do either or both of these in a specific case.

The thin line between judicial incompetence and a judge gone bad is a fuzzy one, then. But so is the line between murder in the first degree, murder in the second degree, voluntary manslaughter, and involuntary manslaughter. We leave it to the criminal process to produce the pertinent facts on what intent, if any, or extenuating circumstances, may have existed. Whether a judge breached his oath with malice in a specific case (or in many) must be determined in a courtroom, after thorough investigation and thoughtful indictment. That a judge has generally discriminated against some group of people may be indicated by statistics. But we would need to find out whether his behavior was related to any personal biases of his. This should be a matter of special investigation by law enforcement officers to see if there is probable cause to bring criminal charges.

The point is that delicate lines of criminal intent do exist throughout American jurisprudence. What must be accepted, because it is demonstrably true, is that such judicial crimes of prejudice may be committed in the courtroom. Once this is clear, we are on the way to passing a law against them. It is inexcusable to refuse to promulgate such a law on the flimsy basis that the line would be too difficult to draw. It is difficult with nonofficial outlaws as well. But officials do not hesitate to do it with those outside government.

OUR TRIAL BALLOON

Actually Americans would be less tiresome if their trial system worked as advertised. Americans spend too much time touting the merits of their way of doing legal business, applauding its maximization of "efficiency," "democracy," and "justice." But woe is us, for the evidence mounts that entire sections of the American system collapse when they touch heat. The American trial system is thus like any trial balloon: hot air inflates it and real heat explodes it.

The analogy to combustion is not gratuitous. One series of events that exposed inherent weaknesses in the system was the urban riots of the middle sixties. Numerous illegal procedures were committed routinely and sanctimoniously by judges, all of which resulted in the substantial intentional deprivation of "in-alienable" rights of countless Americans, most of whom were black. For example, many judges summarily promulgated "preventive detention acts" against entire black communities. Cloaked by the flowing mantles of "judicial discretion," it worked through a misuse of the bail system.

Bail, as nearly everyone knows, allows those with spare cash to extricate themselves from jail pending trial. If one can't raise sufficient funds, one remains a guest of the state. The justification for such clear-cut inequity goes this way: in America, a man is presumed innocent until proven guilty in a court of law, after a full trial. Since it takes time between arrest and judgment, and jail is itself punishment, to permit a suspect to remain free until trial, but ensure his presence at his trial, he must post money, subject to forfeiture if he decides to play fugitive. This system makes some sense despite the fact it favors the wealthy. It makes *some* sense.

The real catch comes in the amount of bail the judge sets for a suspect. The judge is supposed to make this determination on the basis of two major facts: the severity of the crime and the likelihood that this particular man will skip town before trial. In setting bail, the judge must limit his consideration of all facts to the risk that the individual suspect might become a no-show. If a judge considers a suspect's group affiliation or external conditions (a riot is raging outside), he is acting beyond the judicial role for bail proceedings and has become a combination legislator-prosecutor-policeman-judge, beyond the law, beyond his role. Such behavior on his part resulting in further imprisonment, whatever the rationale ("the man may be dangerous to society"), is tantamount to false imprisonment.

Jerome Skolnik, an American sociologist of the upper crust, was commissioned to study the causes and effects of American urban violence, particularly that of 1965-68. His staff collected roomsful of anecdotes and raised mountains of statistics. All were sifted, interpreted, and eventually published in book form as *The Politics of Protest*,[5] with one chapter entitled "Judicial Response in Crisis"—a magnanimous heading, given the sordid facts. A better title would have been "Judicial Retaliation in Crisis."

Skolnik's group gathered much data on the riots in Newark, Detroit, Baltimore, Chicago, and Washington, D.C., including some of these more staggering items:

Item:

According to an ACLU study in Chicago, the average bail for the charge of burglary under "normal" conditions is $4,300. Bail for the winter "looting" cases ranged from $5,000 to $30,000 with an average of $14,000.

Item:

[In Newark] In determining bond, the courts paid little attention to such criteria as the background of those accused, despite the fact that over 70 per cent of the defendants had not been previously arrested, 83 per cent had never been previously convicted, and about 50 per cent were arrested within six blocks of their homes. . . . Ten days after the riot, there were still 200 people in jail who could not make bond.

What happened, of course, was that judges were preventively detaining people in jail as a riot prophylactic. But even those politicos among us today who are most supportive of passing actual preventive detention laws are positively humble before traditional American jurisprudence, when compared with so many municipal judges during those riotous times. Even the staunchest advocates of preventive detention limit its use—at least provisionally—to those suspects who have a record of previous similar crimes or previous crimes of equal magnitude.

What occurred during our summer riots was that some courts granted total license to police dragnet arrests and reinforced them by dragnet preventive detention. These courts had in effect rewritten a time-honored American adage to read: "Better 90 percent innocent stay in jail than 10 percent potential recidivists go free." If you were arrested, whatever the cause, whatever your status, and whatever your past record (or nonrecord), you had scant opportunity to recoup your liberty in the way and time American law allows, nay, demands.

The court system became a broken-down way station on a railroad that led directly to jail, without passing go. There were no hearings, no lawyers, no bail bondsmen, no time, no deliberations, and only a façade of consideration.

But worst of all, some undetermined number of judges talked and acted like politicians running for office, an odd stance for an umpire when the government was an interested party in the case they were hearing. Once a judge makes general policy statements about a general class of people who are to come before his bench, he disqualifies himself as the umpire he is bound and paid to be. If he then sits in judgment, only he can be judged harshly. Many judges in riot-torn cities, in expressing attitudes incompatible with their sworn objective of being impartial and independent, added an unwelcome and inflammatory dose of lawlessness to a highly inflammable situation.

The Skolnik report is liberally laced with statements made by judges during the riots, making it clear that anyone haled before them would not get a fair hearing. The judges were running scared. To be fair, they were frightened by the severe stress their cities were undergoing: whole blocks on fire, massive looting, and no little bloodshed. They acted as men might in self-defense. Actually, they overreacted, flailing wildly and slugging far more innocents than provocateurs. By issuing public threats, they declared themselves as instruments of repression.

But they were judges, not the mayor, governor, or police chief. They were judges, empowered to hear individual cases against individual men so as to decide their fates on specific evidence. These judges could not legally assume that all men before them were guilty simply because they were arrested and a riot was raging.

In a few short pages of the Skolnik report we find judges

saying (when asked about "preventive detention"): (1) "What do you want me to do—cry crocodile tears for people who take advantage of their city?" (2) (To a man who pleaded not guilty) "Someday you'll learn how order is in Chicago." (3) (To a newspaper) "Looting during a citywide emergency is comparable to grave-robbing." (4) "When a man is sitting on the bench and he's looking out the window and he sees the city afire, big blazes here and there and everywhere, and he sees the people who are supposedly involved, it's very difficult for him to make a real considered judgment." (5) "[I will not release] thugs who would help to further [a] 'take-over-by-violence' plan."

These quotes are simply illustrative of the punitive mentality that characterized so much of America's urban judiciary in those awful days.

There was one case where it seemed to be the clear intent of several judges to break the law, each in his own right (if we can rely on the eyewitness testimony of one of their fellow judges). In this situation, we could have had a "judicial conspiracy."

Item:

The twelve Recorder's Court judges [Detroit] met on the second day of the riot . . . and agreed to set bonds averaging $10,000; some were set as high as $200,000. The *Detroit Free Press* noted that as a result . . . , hundreds of persons were "railroaded through Recorder Court . . . slapped with high bonds and stashed away to await trial." The high bail policy was applied uniformly—ignoring the nature of the charge, family and job status of those arrested, the prior record, and all other factors usually considered in the setting of bail.[6]

Given such statements, plus the statistics on excessive bail, plus the evidence as to the speed and lack of counsel that accompanied the proceedings, Skolnik was forced to conclude that there was "a readiness by courts to lend their support to a system of preventive detention, to become an instrument of political needs relatively unrestrained by considerations of legality." In other words, Skolnik found that the anarchy in these mean times

143

was not on the streets alone. It was also sitting in book-lined chambers, sipping sherry.

Unfortunately (but understandably), there has been no high-powered research commissioned by any wing of the establishment (as was done after the riots) to investigate the possibility that governmentally unpopular groups are also having judicially legislated preventive detention acts passed against them. Perhaps the best single illustration of this type of judicial illegality was the painfully obvious disparity in how two bomb cases were handled in New York City in 1969.

No one with a scintilla of sense wants to inhabit a building that is bombed for any purpose, no matter how worthy and pure the bomber considers his cause. Self-righteousness is no balm for another's pain. So it is readily comprehensible that a judge might see merit in barring or delaying a suspected bomber's return to the streets once he is in custody, even though he has no power to do so. The bail route is often used, and the sums demanded by judges are, in a word, ransom. That's bad enough, but when the system (in New York City) requires very different bail for nearly identical situations, serious questions have to be raised about its bias.

As newspaper zealots may remember, New York suffered a series of building blastings in 1969. Soon the police had the cadre of the New York Black Panther Party under arrest, charged with plotting to generate fire sales in several midtown Manhattan department stores. They were each held on $100,000 bail—more than enough to keep the leaders of the Democratic Party in jail, too.

Many bumper stickers later, a detachment of white bombers was caught red-handed and hauled before the New York courts. They were charged with masterminding an earlier citywide demolition party that had replastered walls, vestibules, and washrooms of the IBM Building, the Chase Manhattan Building, and a few other architectually unremarkable edifices. They were apprehended in the nick of time, depositing a cache of TNT into some empty Army trucks. Their bail was set at only $20,000 per person. One can forgive the Panthers for noticing the difference, particularly when the Panther charge was for "conspiracy" (mere words) and the paler bombardiers were being held for their consummate skills and consummated plans.

The main problem with this kind of judicial discrimination is that it is not the work of one judge. The discrimination here inheres in the wider system. If Judge X had hit each Black Panther for $100,000 and it was also Judge X who had imposed $20,000 on each of the whites, there would be strong evidence of his bias. Instead, we have a situation where no one man's behavior, act by act, is involved. Since we have several judges acting at different times, it is harder to find the malice for an act of official anarchy. The anarchism is systemic, not systematic. It still adds up to lawlessness from the victims' viewpoint.

But the clearest cases of overt, individualistic judicial banditry are some of the political "trials" that seem to occur these days in America. I limit myself to the more notorious examples in recent years, since these are, by definition, the ones receiving the widest coverage in the media.

Occasionally, a small-time case reaches the news media, like that of Robert Johnson, a young black civil rights worker in Mississippi, in January 1971. Apparently, the judge in that case made his feelings about the parties and the lawyers perfectly clear. Early in the Johnson trial, Judge Perry stated his belief that civil rights workers were prosocialist and pro-Communist agitators. He also noted, in open court, that the lawyers in these cases were "90 percent Jews." [7] Judge Perry's personal beliefs would seem to provide some evidence that he might find it difficult to be fair, and it could cast some suspicion about his impartiality in meting out a summary contempt citation against the defendant.

Four more prominent illustrations were the "trials" of Dr. Spock, LeRoi Jones, the Chicago Eight Minus One, and Officer O'Brien in San Francisco.

THE PEOPLE OF THE ENEMY AND DR. SPOCK

Francis J. W. Ford was a judge of the Federal District Court of the United States. According to all reports, he typified the veritable backbone of New England plutocracy. He was, in all probability, a judge of the people, well known as a hard-working and dedicated judge, a man with years of experience on the bench. His integrity? Beyond reproach. His pride in his profession was more than evident to anyone in even remote contact with the man. The very model of a gentleman, he was an eighty-five-year-old judge of judges. But as many political scientists, sociologists, psychologists, lawyers, judges, and philosophers of the law have noted, he was naught but a man.

Judge Ford was assigned to preside at the government's case against the so-called Boston Five, who were charged with conspiracy to "counsel, aid, and abet" draftable youths to hinder and interfere with the "Military Selective Service Act of 1967." This was a unique case since the government avoided any allegation that these men *did* anything specifically to accomplish this purpose, that is, that they actually counseled, aided, and abetted. The government stated only that, in some way, they had *come together* to do this, that in essence, they were in collusion to do this.

The charge being rather unusual, the case attracted national attention. And since some of the defendants were highly prominent Americans, deeply involved in the anti-Vietnam movement (Dr. Spock and Reverend Coffin were the two best known), the white heat of television spotlights fell upon Boston and the courtroom of Judge Ford. The stage was set for a dramatic clash between representatives of an older set of patriotic ideals and a newer set, with all the actors being members of the establishment.

If one of these representatives happened to be the judge, the battle would be rigged and therefore illegal. If Judge Ford was convinced of the charge (indictment) beforehand and presided nonetheless, then he would certainly be in contempt of his own court at least. Under such circumstances, Judge Ford would be a judicial outlaw despite a world of self-righteousness and determination to do good.

The point is that many major reporters and commentators covering that trial felt he was prejudiced from the outset, and *in extremis.* Indeed, the views of these observers and their reportage of the facts add up to an overwhelming case of judicial bias. If reasonably accurate, they would strongly support a charge of judicial anarchy, and perhaps a prosecutional investigation into Judge Ford's private beliefs about the defendants before the trial itself got under way.

For instance, according to Daniel Lang of the *New Yorker,* the judge's temperament during the trial was "cantankerous." Lang substantiates this opinion with a quotation from John Mac-Kenzie's article in the *Washington Post* stating, "The Judge's display of bias . . . deprived the Nation of a trial that was fundamentally fair." MacKenzie also found it necessary to remark that the official transcript failed to portray "the manner in which 85-year-old Judge Francis J. W. Ford showed his disbelief in the defense case and his tolerance for the Government's."

Many other expert observers felt the same way. Perhaps Lang's further elaboration will be helpful:

> The official transcript does not convey the skeptical tone that the Judge employed in addressing the defendants when they denied government allegations. . . . In reading the transcript, one cannot hear his hectoring tone as he urged defense lawyers to "get on" or "go forward" on numerous occasions—something he rarely did to the prosecution.

So much for the tone of the judge's demeanor, which can have serious impact on a jury's view of what is being said on a witness stand. For there were other signs of preconceived judicial prejudice against these five defendants as well. Some were verbal slips; some, legal behavior.

As for verbal slips, Lang relates the following: At one point

Judge Ford became quite peeved with defense counsel. And, as irritated judges often do, he issued a warning about a potential contempt citation. This in itself is neither abnormal nor indicative of pretrial bias by a judge. However, he added, loud enough for the jury to hear, that all this had happened before to an attorney representing Communist clients (the "Dennis Lawyers"). Such information was highly gratuitous and potentially prejudicial, should some jury member who knew about the Dennis case make the short step by innuendo.

Another time, according to Lang, during a colloquy before the judge's bench, Judge Ford was heard to refer to two priests who were witnesses for one of the defendants as "those so-called Roman Catholic priests." "So-called"? There was no evidence of defrocking. The judge's skepticism could have resulted from little else but his disagreement with their political behavior.

Another instance of his dislike of the defendants and all they represented came during another bench conference, one on the admissibility of a young war resister as a witness. The transcript, according to Lang, notes that Judge Ford said, "I hope he has long hair."

Other utterances by the good judge fuel the hunch that he was already personally convinced of the guilt of the Boston Five, and hoped that the jury would be of similar mind. Lang and other observers noticed that the judge made several references to the defendants as "this conspiracy," which was the charge, not the verdict. Calling them by that name, instead of "this alleged conspiracy," tipped off the jury to the judge's conviction. Finally, Lang stated, "The day before he gave the jury its instructions, [Judge Ford] predicted during a bench conference, 'There will be one verdict, and that will be guilty on [a] conspiracy count.'"

As to his legal behavior, there were several important events that make it difficult to believe in the impartiality of Judge Ford. Herbert L. Packer, an eminent law professor from Stanford, commented on one among them. It seems the defense was attempting to get a government witness to admit that "he recognized that the defendants were trying individually to commit a crime in his presence." Proof of this would help discredit the conspiracy charge and force the government to indict on individual acts. The transcript (as quoted by Packer) then read: [8]

> Q: (*by defense attorney Boudin*) You allowed them to come in and served them coffee and then you indicted them?
> JUDGE FORD: Strike it out!
> Q: After the conference ended, were any others present at the conference indicted except for these five defendants?
> JUDGE FORD: Strike it out!
> Q: When you were at law school did *you* ever sign anything similar to the "Call to Resist Illegitimate Authority?
> JUDGE FORD (*making a run at Boudin in his swivel chair*): STRIKE IT OUT! [9]

A judge is supposed to wait for objections from the state before sustaining them. There were no objections before the judge's rulings. In the total context of this case, the judge was boldly usurping the prosecutor's role—which is, sadly, a hallmark of nonindependence and prejudice.

Jessica Mitford's close scrutiny of the transcript led her to a similar conclusion—in this case by showing unequal treatment of similar witnesses by the judge. Judge Ford became cross with one defense witness's extreme care with his own choice of words (when a looser usage could have amounted to criminal confession), but insisted on extreme care with another witness's own words in a different, but like, situation.

The first witness, Professor Seymour Melman, had been called by the defense to establish that another defendant had been invited by Reverend Coffin, one of the "co-conspirators," to participate in a particular act only as an afterthought (thereby undermining the government's contention that that person was a conspirator too). On cross-examination, the prosecutor wanted to know about Professor Melman's own delivery of some draft cards, in a briefcase, to the attorney general. The United States attorney, in questioning Melman, asked Melman if he knew what he was doing at the time. Melman hedged by demanding that the prosecutor be precise; Melman seemed alarmed that he was being implicated. The testimony went as follows: [10]

> THE WITNESS (Melman): I said that I was not in possession of draft cards.
> JUDGE FORD: Did you know there were draft cards in that briefcase?
> THE WITNESS: It was said there were draft cards.
> JUDGE FORD: Do you know that they were?
> THE WITNESS: No sir, I did not with my own eyes see a draft card. I don't know how to recognize one.
> JUDGE FORD: (*now furious*) Wait a minute, were you told that there were draft cards in that briefcase?
> THE WITNESS: There may have been.
> JUDGE FORD: WELL, WERE YOU *TOLD* THERE WERE?
> THE WITNESS: Yes, sir.

Miss Mitford tells of a further colloquy on verbal precision between Professor Melman and Judge Ford regarding the same matter. The prosecutor asked the professor if he saw people cramming draft cards into the briefcase. The professor responded with "They may have." Judge Ford then ordered him "to answer whether or not he saw it." The witness insisted he saw no draft cards and that he wouldn't know how to recognize one. He added quickly, "It's my duty, sir, to speak with exact knowledge for what I know *exactly.*" Miss Mitford noted that the judge replied with some intolerance: "Stop that and answer the question!"

But Judge Ford subsequently betrayed his own knowledge of the difference between knowledge and being told or informed of something or merely seeing something. This time the witness was a defendant, Marcus Raskin, and he was explaining his opposition to the Vietnam War, attempting to justify his actions on trial. At this point, Judge Ford displayed his own expertise on the difference between what someone is told and what someone knows.

THE WITNESS (Raskin): Furthermore, the amount of defoliants used has increased over the past four years by a factor of about five. I further learned that by the late summer of 19 . . .

THE COURT: You were informed.

THE WITNESS: I was informed.

THE COURT: Strike out the word "learned." You were informed. Go ahead.

THE WITNESS: I was informed that by the summer of 1967, forty per cent of those serving in Vietnam were people who were drafted into the armed services. Furthermore, I had also learned—

THE COURT: No, been informed . . .

Where knowing (not just being informed) was tantamount to admission of aiding and abetting a crime, but just being informed of something might absolve the witness from admitting his intent to do a crime, the judge was quite perturbed over the distinction of appearances, spoken information, and knowledge (learning). Where knowing (not just being informed) carried the stamp of the witness's expertise about the Vietnam War, the judge was quite fastidious in forcing the witness to be acutely exact about the difference.

Do so many asides, quasi-prejudicial remarks, verbal slips, and inconsistent legal behaviors call Judge Ford's objective umpiring into serious question? These incidents could have justified full-scale inquiry into Judge Ford's attitudes toward these men, the Vietnam War, and the antiwar movement. And, if any other more direct evidence could be unearthed to support the suspicion of his pretrial prejudices, I should think that an indictment could have been handed down against the judge for depriving the defendants of their civil rights, under the color of law. He might also have been indicted on an attempted kidnapping charge.

THE NEWARK BIG ONE

Though not as legally political in texture as that of the Boston Five, the case against LeRoi Jones in Newark may well have been equally political. It, too, was crammed full with enough facts to cast heavy suspicion about its being a judicial (fair) trial. It may well have been a "political trial."

LeRoi Jones was the leading *bête noire* of many white Newarkers. His poetry and plays brim with hatred of white America. And one would have to be deaf to miss Jones' near-advocacy of violence by black people against white people as an act of moral revenge. Despite his soft tone while speaking, LeRoi Jones carries a very big stick. He may be mellowing with age, but in the late sixties, LeRoi Jones was the apotheosis of a fearful black rage.

It is readily comprehensible why many white Newarkers might be nervous about Jones. His ill will toward them was well understood, and reciprocated. Add to this misalliance the Newark riot of July 1967. It was hot and humid that summer, and the political and social situation in Newark was ripe for big trouble. So when it came, it was one of the worst of its genre. During the riot, parts of Newark were leveled by large numbers of the black community. The situation teetered on insurrection. And LeRoi Jones was there, big as life.

Late one evening during the riots, he was driving through a black ward in his VW camper with a small group of friends. Suddenly the Newark police appeared and pulled them over. A verbal dispute was soon followed by a storm of violence between Jones' group and the Newark Police. Among other charges, Jones was arrested for carrying a concealed weapon.

Judge Leon Kapp is a Newarker who, along with other members of the New Jersey white establishment, took a dim view of the gutting of wide sectors of his city. He, along with other members of the New Jersey white establishment, was determined to punish those responsible for this indelicacy. And there was Jones with the Newark police claiming they had the goods on him.

The stage was set for a trial on ostensibly nonpolitical charges (concealed weapons). But the more the politicians and legal participants denied the political implications of the forthcoming trial, the more obvious their political stake became—particularly if Jones was convicted.

The defense had good reason to fear that a trial in Newark, given the climate then prevailing there, would result in another soul on ice. The defense therefore moved for a change of trial venue to another part of the state, where there might be less white enmity and less political pressure for revenge. According to New Jersey practice, the judge in a case usually hails from the place where the trial is held. So, when the original venue was Newark, Kapp, as an Essex County judge, was assigned. Ordinarily, a judge surrenders a case when its venue is removed to another part of the state. But this was no ordinary case, and Judge Kapp elected to stay with it. With the venue now in suburban Morris County, Newark Judge Kapp was still on the job. And the jury turned out to be snow-white.

From the start, seasoned reporters sensed that the judge had prejudged the case and was hell-bent on conviction. And what was worse, this time he had a teammate in the prosecutor, Andrew Zazzali.

Two political scientists at the University of Wisconsin, Joel Grossman and Kenneth Dolbeare, after conducting a thorough post mortem of this trial, were convinced that Judge Kapp was highly antagonistic toward Jones.[11] According to them, the judge intruded throughout the trial, conducting "interrogations of prosecution witnesses to insure that their damaging statements were clearly heard and understood by the jury." [12]

And, as is so often the case in political trials, the judge openly aired his prejudice during the charge to the jury. The charge is an excellent place for a judge to inject his personal opinion;

for it is there it can be most damaging. It is there that the jury is most dependent on and subservient to judicial expertise. What happened at the Jones trial? According to Grossman and Dolbeare, "At the end of the trial he charged the jury so as to leave no doubt of his belief that Jones was a liar and a scoundrel and the arresting officers were model policemen who had simply been doing their patriotic duty in difficult circumstances." [13]

Among other phrases spicing Judge Kapp's charge were his reference to the Newark policemen as "these five men in blue" and his admonition to the twelve jurors that "the police officer is the shield of the community against the use of violence and other lawless acts." [14] Judge Kapp also made derogatory comments about Jones' defense, speaking of "the mass of trivia which unfortunately has crept into this trial." [15]

The real importance of the Jones case is that it shows how a less celebrated part of a trial can become the focal point for a judge's personal dislike for a defendant and all he stands for. In the Jones trial, after the jury had returned its guilty verdict, the sentence was delayed and read back in Newark.

Again (according to Grossman and Dolbeare), Judge Kapp's "demeanor and tone were perceived by many of the Negroes . . . as thoroughly racist and deliberately provocative." [16] Jones' two codefendants received moderate sentences. One was delivered to the care of the county jail for a year, the other for half that time. One received a fine of $500, the other $250.

Jones, however, had bigger things in store for him. Judge Kapp threw the book, and nearly his gavel, at Jones. He was to be incarcerated for two and a half to three years (the maximum sentence was three years) in the New Jersey State Penitentiary and was denied any possibility of probation (which each of the other two codefendants had received).

But Judge Kapp went even further; he read aloud, for one and all to hear, the reason for his harsh decision. He recited one of several poems Jones had recently published in *Evergreen*

Review, but after the trial was over: it was the famous paragraph that began: "Black People!"

> All the stores will open if you will say the magic words. The magic words are: Up against the wall mother fucker this is a stick up! Or: Smash the window at night (these are magic actions) smash the windows daytime, anytime, together, let's smash the window, drag the shit from in there. No money down. No time to pay. Just take what you want.[17]

This was read to the court, by the judge, who inserted the word "blank" for such words as "mother fucker" and "shit." But Jones was not being tried for his poetry. He was tried for illegal possession of weapons. Some journalists noted that this cast doubt on the real nature of the trial. *Ramparts* said it was obvious that Judge Kapp had "no respect for the law," and demanded his impeachment.[18] *Newsweek* observed that "it was plain that Kapp had indeed held Jones' poetry against him"; [19] and the *New York Times* was incensed at the judge's behavior at the trial, but particularly at the sentencing.[20]

Finally, though, Kapp was reversed by the Superior Court of New Jersey, mainly on the basis of his charge.[21]

Very strong expert opinion (professors, journalists, and jurists) supported the contention that Judge Kapp had let his own strong hostility toward Jones get the better of his judicious temperament. If they were correct, Judge Kapp was a perfect example of a judicial outlaw who forfeited all claim to his position.

If there were such strong opinion that he had been guilty of some other malefaction, like embezzlement or bribery, great establishment pressures would have been brought to bear for investigation and for indictment. But our system does not work that way yet. Up to now we seem to care only if judicial lawlessness was designed to rob another man of his money, not if it was designed to rob him of three years of his life and freedom.

THE SQUARE ROOT OF JUDGE HOFFMAN

If Judge Ford represented one corner of the white establishment against an ungrateful white counterelite, and Judge Kapp represented the entrenched white establishment against an emerging black revolution, then Julius Hoffman and the Chicago Eight Minus One represent another classic conflict in modern-day America. It was the clash of the Squares versus the Counterculture, and the criminal guise for this struggle was a new federal act passed in 1968. The main charge was conspiracy to cross state lines to cause trouble.

Had the Square Establishment scoured America for a hero, they couldn't have done better than Judge Hoffman. First, he was a super-relic of a bygone era. Second, he was a martinet, demanding military discipline and deference in his courtroom. And third, he had as dry a sense of comedy and drama as the defendants and their attorneys. Some even thought he had a comic appearance (the *Village Voice* said he looked like a "dehydrated Elmer Fudd").

Judge Hoffman's rancor toward the defendants and their legal staff did not take long to surface. As soon as the lawyers for the defense were announced (they practiced in California, New Jersey, and New York), Judge Hoffman asked: "These men are taking bread out of the mouths of our Chicago Bar here?" [22]

Shortly thereafter, Jerry Rubin was asked to plead and his counsel, William Kunstler, began by saying "Just for the record—." Judge Hoffman stopped him cold. "Everything we do is for the record," said the judge. "That is why the government pays a high salary for an official reporter. I am not frightened when you say 'for the record.'" Kunstler replied that he was not trying to intimidate the court with his remark, and the judge replied: "Perhaps even way out in New York you have found that I don't frighten easily." [23] The die was cast.

For starters, Judge Hoffman denied a motion that the trial be postponed for six months so that defense counsel might have more adequate time to prepare the complex case. Then four other lawyers, claiming they had been retained only for pretrial motions, wired the court their desire to be relieved of their duties. They were back in their home states. Judge Hoffman, demanding their formal presence to rule upon their self-removal from the case, found them in contempt of court. Some came to Chicago voluntarily and one in handcuffs. Judge Hoffman ordered all held—involuntarily, without bail, in jail, over the weekend—until sentencing. This was rather stern treatment for lawyers who wished only to leave a case.

Hoffman's judicial behavior was immediately denounced by the National Lawyers Guild and the ACLU, and a swelling discontent burst into a massive rally by lawyers in the courthouse protesting the judge's action. Apparently, this unexpected response by so many lawyers, in person, from all over the country, helped Judge Hoffman reverse himself. It was now perfectly clear to many observers that this was going to be quite a trial.

The next indicator of judicial prejudice in the conspiracy trial was Judge Hoffman's legal treatment of the medical illness of Charles R. Garry. Mr. Garry is a white attorney from San Francisco who has long been the chief counsel of the Black Panther Party. Black Panthers are not known to get along famously with too many white men, but Mr. Garry has gained their ultimate confidence as their counsel. He had been appointed to defend Bobby Seale, the BPP's chairman, one of the original Chicago Eight.

Shortly after the trial began, Garry became ill and was strongly urged to have his gall bladder removed. The hospitalization was to take several weeks. Garry asked for a postponement of the trial; Judge Hoffman refused. Under the circumstances, the request seemed reasonable and *bona fide;* the denial appeared unreasonable and in bad faith. Judge Hoffman did little to indicate that the appearance did not match the reality.

So the trial got under way with only Kunstler and Leonard Weinglass to counsel all eight defendants. Bobby Seale sat patiently, quietly, through the long jury selection. After the jury was sworn in, Seale called San Francisco to find out whether Garry would be in Chicago the next day to defend him. The answer was no. The next day at the trial, Seale "fired" Kunstler and Weinglass and demanded a postponement of his trial until Garry's return. Judge Hoffman denied this request, too.

It is an important tenet of American law that a man is entitled to counsel of his choice, particularly if he can afford his services. It is equally well settled that a man can represent himself. Judge Hoffman could have severed the Seale case until Garry returned, and he could have allowed Bobby Seale to handle his own case as co-counsel, along with Kunstler and Weinglass. In any event, Seale constantly attempted to act in this capacity throughout his daily visits to the courtroom. But the judge was determined to run his courtroom in strict accordance with his own incredibly narrow interpretation of the rules. If that meant that the frustration level of the defense might be raised to a point of disruption, the judge was prepared to treat that rigidly and vengefully. It did, and he did.

As far as Seale was concerned, the denial of his plea to have his case postponed and to be allowed to plead his own case was more than enough to convince him that he was destined for a spell behind bars. Perhaps that was not a substantial enough set of indicators to establish *objectively* that a judge is biased toward someone. But it's plain to see that it could look that way to one up on a conspiracy charge (when he had met only one of his seven coconspirators before his trial), and who feels that the system is out to get him.

If one is so convinced, one would see the trial as a sham trial and the judge as a sham judge. Once that is concluded, one can subjectively commit no contempt of court. Also, he might feel it essential to manifest substantial contempt of the sham court. For in his eyes, a contempt of the sham is an affirmation of genuine "courtness" and real justice. This seems to be the heart of the Hoffman-Seale comedy, a few lines of which illustrate this point: [24]

MR. SEALE: Hey, you [Weinglass] don't speak for me. I would like to speak of my own self and have my counsel handle my case in behalf of myself. How come I can't speak in behalf of myself? I am my own legal counsel. I don't want my lawyers to represent me.

THE COURT: You have a lawyer of record, and he has been of record here for you since September 24.

MR. SEALE: I have been arguing that before that jury heard one shred of evidence. I don't want these lawyers because I can take up my own legal defense, and my lawyer is Charles Garry.

THE COURT: I direct you, sir, to remain quiet.

MR. SEALE: And just be railroaded?

THE COURT: Will you remain quiet?

MR. SEALE: I want to defend myself, do you mind, please?

THE COURT: Let the record show that the defendant Seale continued to speak after the Court courteously requested him to remain quiet.

Another representative interchange between the two (Item No. 6 in the contempt citation against Seale):

MR. SEALE: [*Objecting to Government's Exhibit 14, which was being described by U.S. Attorney Schultz as depicting a boy giving the "black power" sign.*] That's not a black power sign. Somebody correct the Court on that. It's not the black power sign. It's the power to the people sign.

THE COURT: Mr. Marshal, will you stop the talking, please.

MR. SEALE: Yes, but that is still wrong, Judge Hoffman. It's not a black power sign. It's a power to the people sign, and he is deliberately distorting that and that's a racist technique.

MR. SCHULTZ: If the Court please, this man has repeatedly called me a racist.

MR. SEALE: Yes, you are. You are Dick Schultz.

MR. SCHULTZ: And called Mr. Foran a racist.

THE COURT: Ladies and gentlemen of the jury, I will ask you to leave the Court . . .

(They leave)

The following proceedings were had in open court, out of the presence and hearing of the jury:

THE COURT: Mr. Seale and Mr. Kunstler, your lawyer, I must admonish you that such outbursts are considered by the Court to be contemptuous, contumacious, and will be dealt with appropriately in the future.

MR. KUNSTLER: Your Honor, the defendant was trying to defend himself, and I have already indicated my—

THE COURT: The defendant was not defending himself.

MR. SEALE: I was, too, defending myself. Any time anybody gives me the wrong symbol in this courtroom is deliberately—

THE COURT: He is not addressing me with authority—

MR. SEALE:—distorting, and put it on the record.

THE COURT: Instruct that man to keep quiet.

MR. SEALE: I want to defend myself and ask him if he isn't lying, and he is going to put that lying crap on the record. No, sirree—I am not going to sit here and get that on the record. I am going to at least let it be known—request that you understand that this man is erroneously representing symbols directly related to the party of which I am chairman.

(And even while bound and gagged) . . .

MR. SEALE: (*through his gag*) I would like to cross-examine the witness. I want to cross-examine the witness.

THE COURT: Ladies and gentlemen of the jury, I will have to excuse you.

MR. SEALE: My constitutional rights have been violated. The direct examination is over, cross-examination is over, I want to cross-examine the witness.

THE COURT: Please be quiet, sir. I order you to be quiet. . . . You sat there and did not during this afternoon intrude into the proceedings in an improper way.

MR. SEALE: I never intruded until it was the proper time for me to ask and request and demand that I have a right to

160

defend myself and I have a right to cross-examine the witness.

(This exchange was in Item 15 of the bill of particulars against Seale.)

With these highly publicized incidents in the early stages of the trial, the scene was set for even worse displays of judicial distemper.

I journeyed to Chicago in December 1969 to test the atmosphere. With the help of Mr. Weinglass, and through the good offices of one of the marshals, I managed to get into the courtroom. By that time, the scenario was well into Act Two. Bobby Seale was long gone, but the distrust and sarcasm between the judge and the defense were thick enough to feel. I've never sensed such blatant contempt by a judge toward a lawyer (Kunstler) and, I might add, the two days I was there were very, *very* dull days.

Meanwhile, the "conspiracy" cavorted at the defense table, rustling about, whispering, snickering, passing notes, unkempt (except for Dellinger), delighting in their temporary immunity. Judge Hoffman never glanced their way. He reserved his acrimony for their advocates. Judge Hoffman, the square root of the difficulties heaped upon Abbie Hoffman, Jerry Rubin, Tom Hayden, and the rest, had fallen prey to their taunts, and had abandoned even a bare pretense of neutrality toward them.

No one can deny that Federal District Court Judge Julius Hoffman was subjected to as saturating a barrage of abuse as any judge has had to tolerate in his own courtroom. Questions of causation aside, he was pilloried and castigated from the beginning to the end of the trial. He was frequently called a racist (mainly by Bobby Seale) and a fascist (by nearly everyone).

But it was Abbie Hoffman who tried hardest to sting Judge Hoffman in his most vulnerable parts. The younger Hoffman knew the older Hoffman prided himself on being Jewish. He orally compared the judge to Hitler, and at one point called him a "runt" (Judge Hoffman is only five feet four inches tall) who was a "disgrace to the Jews." He also publicly called him a "Shonda fur de Goyem," which he translated as a "front man for the WASP power elite."

It became clear that at some point in the trial the Chicago Seven embarked on a strategy to turn the trial into a farce. Norman Mailer described it well. Their plan, he said, was to surround the fortress and make faces at everyone inside. This would cause the defenders to have nervous breakdowns and destroy themselves.

The tactics included:

On Bobby Seale's birthday, the Chicago Seven brought a cake to the courtroom, which the marshals took from them at the door. Rennie Davis shouted: "They have arrested the cake, Bobby. They arrested it."

Then there was the toilet incident, when the Seven managed to debate Judge Hoffman over which bathroom they could use.

Another incident planned to provoke the judge was to smuggle a Vietcong flag into the courtroom and drape it over their table. As Judge Hoffman entered, defendant Dellinger arose, wearing a black armband and announced: "Mr. Hoffman, we are observing the Moratorium."

As the *coup de grâce,* they made a motion for adjournment so the Seven could participate in a march to protest the "police assassination" of two Chicago Black Panthers (December 1969).

The war for "courtness" was being waged, and American justice could only lose if the judge lost his composure. Any judge has weapons at his disposal. But Judge Hoffman was not inclined to be either subtle or restrained. He was an angry man. And he was convinced that it was right and just to vent his anger and disgust in the courtroom against all of the defendants, many of their witnesses, and both of the attorneys of record. He did this by intermittent sarcasm, by rebuking them all before the jury, and by flagrantly prejudicial rulings on some critical evidence.

Some more unprecedented examples of unjudicious behavior follow.

Judge Hoffman predicted in open court that the two lawyers would receive prison sentences at the end of the trial. This could have been done privately, if it was meant only to deter them. Being done openly, it could only have the extra effect of influencing the jurors against the lawyers.

He openly rebuked Weinglass for speaking "offensively" to one of the prosecutors. When U.S. Attorney Thomas Foran called Kunstler a "mouthpiece" in open court, however, the judge said, "I will ignore it," a telltale inconsistency in the judge's behavior.

He cautioned Kunstler to avoid leaning against the lectern while speaking. Said the judge in open court: "It looked as if you were having a beer. I think it's slovenly." Again, such warnings and admonitions could have been administered in the judge's chambers. In open court, they carried a potential to prejudice.

Despite his remarkable memory, Judge Hoffman constantly mispronounced Counsel Weinglass' name. He called him "Weinron," "Feinglass," "Weinstein," "Feinstein" regularly. It may not have been intentional nor a blatant indicator of his personal scorn for an officer of the court. But it seems so.

When Norman Mailer was on the stand attempting to describe the wide gap in viewpoints between various factions of the new left, particularly on disadvantages to the use of violence (after all, the mutual, concurrent intent of the defendants to cause violence was the core of the government's case), Judge Hoffman was not reluctant to harry him. At one point during his testimony, Mailer was trying to embroider his response when Judge Hoffman told him: "You are too high-priced a writer to give us all that gratis, Mr. Mailer. Just answer the question."

Subsequently, Assistant U.S. Attorney Schultz objected to Mailer's flowery language. Judge Hoffman shot back: "Yes, we're simple folks here. Tell us what you said and he said."

Worst of all was the uneven hand of the judge in ruling on

admissibility of evidence in the defense's case. These seven men were on trial for "intent" to travel to Chicago in order to incite violence. Consequently, much of the defense's case had to rely on testimony that this was certainly not their intent *before* arriving in Chicago. The best single instance of how Judge Hoffman castrated this defense point occurred when former U.S. Attorney General Ramsey Clark tried to testify on behalf of the Chicago Seven, on behalf of their peaceful intentions prior to the convention.

When Clark was introduced as a defense witness, the U.S. attorney objected that much of his testimony might violate U.S. government regulations prohibiting disclosure of Justice Department files, in addition to "other security matters." Clark then took the stand, before the jury's arrival, and tried to answer a series of questions put to him by Kunstler. Many were objected to, particularly those concerning what happened at a Cabinet meeting. Nearly every objection was sustained by Judge Hoffman. Soon after, Judge Hoffman barred the former U.S. Attorney General from taking the stand altogether. The jury remained totally ignorant of the fact that this high Johnson administration official had come to vouch for the defense's major contention.

According to J. Anthony Lukas' account in the *New York Times*, Mr. Clark was willing to testify as follows:

> In answer to one of the questions that were allowed, Mr. Clark said he telephoned Mayor Richard J. Daley of Chicago on July 25, 1968, to set up an appointment with him for Roger Wilkins, then an Assistant Attorney General.
> He said Mr. Wilkins later told him that his conversation with the Mayor was "not very satisfactory" and that Mr. Daley was "not very conciliatory."
> In contrast, Mr. Clark said, Mr. Wilkins was "favorably impressed" by Rennie Davis, one of the demonstration leaders, who [was] a defendant. . . .

The crucial issue at this trial was: Who was the proximate cause of violence in Chicago, the demonstrators or the police (in collusion with the city administration)? The evidence Clark was willing to present could have been weighty indeed in establishing a "reasonable doubt" in the minds of the jury that any criminal intent had been formulated by the defendants in advance of their journey to Chicago. Much of the government's case rested on statements by the defendants advocating violence after they were in Chicago. Such an intent to do violence while in Chicago could have been formulated after initial sallies with the police. Yet these statements by the Seven while in Chicago were admissible.

The *New York Times* on its editorial page referred to the Ramsey Clark incident as an "extraordinary maneuver" in refusing to "let the jury hear pertinent testimony." It went on to say that "when even the man who headed the Justice Department at the time of the demonstration is barred from taking the stand, it is fair to ask whether these proceedings constitute a jury trial at all." [25] Tom Hayden has detailed many other aspects of the defense case that were relevant to the "Conspiracy's" state of mind before coming to Chicago, but that Judge Hoffman refused to let the jury hear.[26]

One of the "Conspiracy's" main points was that the trial had been set up to get them out of the way for as long as possible. Judge Hoffman's behavior during the trial helped establish the credibility of that contention. His actions after the guilty verdict was reached made that point seem all but gospel. First, he initially refused to allow bail for any of them, and did so only when compelled to by a higher court. Clearly, he wished to hold them in jail even if they could put up the money—which he knew they could. Next, he violated the letter and spirit of Federal District Court practice in sentencing Bobby Seale for contempt.

On November 5, 1969, Judge Hoffman announced his sentence for the Black Panther chairman. (Keep in mind that Seale had yet to be tried and convicted for any alleged crime, and had asked that his trial be severed all along.) Judge Hoffman decided finally to sever Seale's case, but also to imprison him on sixteen counts of contempt of court for four years! (Each count was for three months.)

Now, there has been a long-standing rule on the length of contempt sentences. According to Alan Dershowitz, a professor at Harvard Law School, there was "no case in the entire history of Anglo-American jurisprudence in which a sentence of this length has been handed out for criminal contempt." Dershowitz noted that he knew of only one contempt sentence that had been as long as three years, and that had been for jumping bail, so such a lengthy sentence is understandable.

Ronald Goldfarb, an acknowledged expert on the contempt power (and author of a book called *The Contempt Power* [27]), observed that the Supreme Court once ruled that in a case of summary contempt (when there is no trial by jury on a contempt charge), a trial judge can give no more than a six-month sentence. Goldfarb noted, however, that the Supreme Court had never ruled on the question of whether a judge could separate counts and pile up charges of less than six months to run consecutively. But he also observed that the courts have forbidden judges to pile up successive refusals of a witness to answer questions as separate counts of contempt.

In any event, this revolutionary action by Judge Hoffman, coupled with his extraordinary treatment of the trial lawyers in another contempt citation, probably established the all-time American record of time in jail for contempt in one trial. Both Kunstler and Weinglass received two years in jail for contempt of court, with Hoffman noting that it was their duty to restrain their clients, a questionable and novel point of law. The square root of Judge Hoffman was indeed a radical sign.

If ever a judge amassed a record of actions that amounted to more than a reasonable suspicion of malice aforethought, it was Judge Hoffman at the Chicago conspiracy trial. What is the worst this system as presently constituted would do to Judge Hoffman, if a higher court concluded that he was indeed responsible for the prejudice suggested above? Why, reverse the convictions. That's all. Such is the swift and sharp retribution that our system visits on judicial anarchists—once they are exposed, if they are ever exposed.

SILENCE IS YELLOW

But it is unnecessary for judges to be so active in manifesting overt bias in a case. Sometimes they permit a lawyer to do it for them, by abstaining from keeping the level of prejudice pollution at an emotion-laden trial at a bare minimum. The best reported example of this, for what it is worth, described in *Ramparts* magazine, was a trial that took place in San Francisco in 1969.

The facts as reported were roughly as follows: Michael O'Brien, an officer on the San Francisco police force, was off duty, on a date with a woman. O'Brien was in a black section of town that evening, and ended up killing a young black man. Black people in the area testified that he had three black men against a wall when George Basset attacked him with a short slat of a stick. As he was backing away, O'Brien shot Basset dead.

The impression of all the black witnesses was that O'Brien was either blind with hatred of Negroes (one witness testified that he shouted at the three against the wall, "I want to kill a nigger so goddamned bad I can taste it") or blind drunk. There was a young white witness, named David Anderson, who verified most of the black testimony. According to Officer O'Brien's defense, he was viciously attacked by Basset and was falling away from Basset's attack when his gun discharged accidentally.

If the jury believed O'Brien, they should have acquitted him, as he would have been guilty of involuntary manslaughter, having acted in self-defense. If they believed the prosecution's witnesses, they should have convicted him of at least voluntary manslaughter, with no self-defense, and probably should have convicted him of at least murder in the second degree. It was pretty much a case of whom the jury believed on the stand.

The judge's name was Joseph Karesh, and he was considered locally to be a political liberal. The defense lawyer was named Jake Ehrlich. The following are points from the transcript, reported in *Ramparts*. Remember that this was a murder trial, and that lawyers are obligated to refrain from racist remarks during any trial, and that lawyers should try to confine their remarks during summation to what has been offered as proof in evidence.

At the beginning of the trial, Ehrlich noted that a key issue was "this black-white entanglement." Race was not at issue, and bringing it up was worse than irrelevant; it was prejudicial. *Ramparts* noted, "Judge Karesh found nothing to criticize in that formulation."

A black man named Hawkins testified that O'Brien coolly fired his gun at the victim. The dead man's brother corroborated this. Ehrlich called him a "professional liar." This was objected to by the prosecuting attorney as being a "disgusting" phrase. It was more than that; it was not substantiated and it was prejudicial. Judge Karesh "let Ehrlich rant."

David Anderson took the stand. Ehrlich spent much time on him, emphasizing and reemphasizing the fact that he was a student at San Francisco State. Anderson had to repeatedly deny any connection between himself and SDS, the Black Panther Party, and many viewpoints held by various radical factions at San Francisco State. Although Ehrlich produced no evidence to contradict Anderson's position, he felt free to state at one point: "This is a white and black fight. . . . This man Anderson is an unmitigated liar. Any man who would sit there and lie a man's life away is not entitled to a fair trial—he should be taken out and shot." (Anderson was not on trial; Ehrlich's client was.) *Ramparts* noted, "For this bit of legal theory from the city's foremost legal attorney, the judge had not one word of rebuke."

Mr. Ehrlich commenced his summary by noting that the street

where the incident occurred was "a hellhole, with two hundred hyenas in there." He attacked Mayor Joseph Alioto for "ordering" the trial. The veracity of both these statements was highly questionable. Ehrlich referred to Hawkins, the black witness, as "Mr. Holier-Than-Thou," "Old Mr. Prayer Meeting," and the "Deacon." As for Anderson, the following polemic was reserved for him: "This boy is a member of SDS and hates police as sure as I'm standing here. He hates them and would shoot them if he had a chance. . . . [He] is a vicious young punk who wants to destroy our government . . . our homes, our children, two hundred years of American democracy and the flag and all that stands for."

Enough. The judge, according to the report, sat mute. If all this is true, it would seem difficult to commend him for his impartiality in remaining silent. Officer O'Brien was acquitted. Sometimes silence is not golden—it is yellow. A judge can act far beyond the legal demands of his role by refusing to stop outrages in his courtroom. And, if a pattern is established, one can conclude that the judge became a party to a contempt of his own court.

Of course judges can be outlaws. And why not? They are like the rest of us—subject to insidious predilections that tempt us all to perfidy. Some of us fail, judges included. So, whether they end up as self-appointed legislators, *ad hoc* police chiefs, judicial conspirators, amass unenviable records of discrimination against some out-group, or crumple into judicial anarchy at a specific trial, the facts are plain for all to see, once one admits that it can happen here.

We must not shrink from facing this harsh political reality squarely. We must soberly and solemnly consider measures of prevention and retaliation against judicial renegades. We owe it to the innocents among us.

And POGONOGO would be the most creditable banker for that debt.

7

Local Official
Anarchy

"I understand it."

"No you don't. Every man's supposed to have certain inalienable rights."

"Certain inalienable rights," Starke said, "to liberty, equality, and the pursuit of happiness. I learnt it in school as a kid."

"Not that," Prew said. "That's the Constitution. Nobody believes that anymore."

"Sure they do," Starke said. "They all believe it. They just don't do it. But they believe it."

"Sure," Prew said. "That's what I mean."

—*From Here to Eternity*

A few years ago, I lived in a beach town on the West Coast. Let's call it Seabird. Since Seabird was haven to an art community, its economy was closely linked to attracting tourists. As long as the tourists came, milled, and browsed, its many restaurants, gasoline stations, and boutiques flourished. Most of Seabird's potential income, then, rested in the clutches of older, middle-class residents of Southern California.

The government of this town, like local governments everywhere, was a tool of the economy, so protecting property was one of its major roles. Some criminal laws directly relate to property protection (burglary, trespassing), some are indirectly related to property values (loitering, vagrancy), and some seem to bear even less relation to it (possession of marijuana).

This town is a very pretty setting. It holds great allure for young people as well as older ones. As America's school population takes to the road each summer, large bands of them straggle through the main drag of Seabird. Since they don't own property, and can't afford to join country clubs, they establish their own points of contact for each other; they find and populate certain places—some public, some not so public, some private—and spend much time commuting from one hub to another.

The immaculate thoroughfares of Seabird gradually accumulated more and more than the town's fair share of counterculturists sitting around, talking, looking content (that happy smile), and taking surf breaks. Consequently, more and more of the middle-aged, middle-class, middle-road society of Southern California shunned Seabird. The town was acquiring a reputation as "hippie"; despite the absence of detour signs, Seabird was being given a wide berth. The wheels of the economy were beginning to grind, creak, and slow down.

HOW TO ALIENATE INALIENABLE RIGHTS

The decline in business and the flouting of laws were trends the local elite could not help noticing. Seabird needed some law and order. So the police began a heavy crackdown. The young, the oddly clad, and those not known to be related to someone in town were stopped, quizzed, and sometimes frisked by the local constabulary. Repression might be an unfair characterization, but harassment would not.

The "daily hassle" was on. Looking for relaxation, kids found tension; seeking community, they found government. Seabird was dumping on them, and it was not aiming to please. I do not mean to suggest that the business elite met one evening with the mayor and the police and decided to purge the youth. Even if they did, that would have been fine, as long as they didn't plan to enforce laws selectively. Vagrancy laws have long been considered valid, although they have recently run afoul of some enlightened Supreme Courts, and officials still classify marijuana as a narcotic. So there was a well-stocked legal arsenal that local officials intended to use in their war against youthful poverty. But one procedure adopted pointed strongly to an illegal collusion among police, the prosecutor's office, and a local judge.

In order to speed the successful conclusion of any military campaign, it helps to enlist even the unwitting cooperation of the enemy. One way of doing that is to find and exploit its weakness. A citizen's ignorance of his civil rights has always been a staple of police procedure, particularly when police departments feel pressured to accomplish some mission rapidly.

Now, all educated Americans know that the Fourth Amendment of the United States Constitution guarantees every American freedom against unreasonable search. And American jurisprudence makes it very clear that police cannot enjoy so-called fishing expeditions and search or arrest everyone who fits into a class of people (blacks, longhairs, demonstrators) merely because more people in those groups commit certain crimes than people in other groups and classes.

A policeman must have "probable cause" to suspect that a particular person is committing a specific crime at that immediate time in order to justify a search and/or arrest. But in Seabird the search became an end in itself. Police searches are never gentle and are always degrading and humiliating to the searched. The more real the threat of a search became, the more desirable it became for people who were likely to be searched to abandon the town—which was exactly what many Seabirds wanted.

Teen-agers have at least as little expertise on the Constitution as most people, if not less. So it was easy for local officials to prepetrate a gigantic hoax upon them. What was done was simple enough. Once a youth was "busted" for any crime, but particularly for possession of marijuana, he was advised to plead guilty, and if he did, was guaranteed a suspended sentence. However, the probation had a catch to it. One feature of the probationary period was that the youngster was compelled to "waive his Fourth Amendment rights."

Imagine that in America. A prosecutor and a judge in league together to advise young Americans that they could and should surrender their inalienable rights under the American Constitution. What this amounted to, quite simply, was that policemen, who knew of such a waiver, could walk up to such rightless persons, and search them at will. The policeman, now a co-conspirator along with prosecutor and judge, was an accomplice to rob people of their right to privacy. The policeman wouldn't have to suspect one of these rightless creatures of anything. He could search at his leisure, as often as he liked. The victim remained unaware of his right to resist, since a judge had pretended that such a right could be abandoned.

It is difficult to say who was more alienated from the American system at that time, the young man who believed that it could be that way, or the prosecutor, judge, and police, who wanted to make it so.

Many contemporary young people, with their outrageous costuming and posturing, find it very difficult to avoid uneven application of law and flagrant violations of the law by local officials acting together. There has been a surge of this kind of local conspiracy in the last few years, particularly in relation to the promoting, staging, and enjoyment of rock music festivals. Officials of local communities have a bottomless bag of illegal tricks to keep the new barbarians at bay. "Live and let live" is not guaranteed by the United States Constitution, but protection against a systematic distortion and discriminatory application of existing law is.

It has become commonplace to read newspaper stories that reek of collusion among local officials to run people in, keep them incarcerated as long as possible, or deport them on the next Greyhound.

Item:

"Governor Claude R. Kirk, Jr., paid a call today on thousands of youths massed for a weekend rock festival near West Palm Beach and ordered one of them arrested. The Governor said that he would not let Florida become a playground for hippies." [1]

How could one governor do all this himself? He could not. The governor could only accomplish this premeditated violation of American law with the cooperation of government officials throughout the state to selectively enforce statutes against "hippie" elements polluting Florida's life-space.

As further proof of the seriousness with which he meant his statement to be taken and of the necessity to recruit other elements of local government, consider the following incident. Governor Kirk asked a "long-haired youth" how he felt. The lad replied "pretty good." When the governor asked where the young man hailed from, the hippie refused to answer. The governor had only one recourse. He took it. "Take him," he said. Kirk waved at Sheriff William Heidtman, who ordered two of his deputies to spirit the offensive hippie off in a squad car—which they dutifully did. There was no comment on charges other than a few choice words by the governor. He made the nature of the charges perfectly clear: "These kids think they can play in Florida. Well, they are wrong. You can't play anywhere in this state or in Palm Beach County."

The governor had summarily passed a novel law against playing around. It was duly ratified by a sheriff and two deputies. A new branch of anarchy was born.

During the summer of 1970, the Great Antirock Conspiracy started to roll. As far as rock fetes were concerned, local officialdom was fast turning antibusiness.

Ingenious methods were devised to undermine such phenomena through "legal" means. Some areas, fearing an injection of summer youth into their winter veins, passed public health laws that made it unfeasible and unprofitable for a promoter to try to stage a concert in the immediate area.

During the summer of 1970, the following also happened: Governor Lester Maddox of Georgia called for legislation to ban pop festivals in his state; a promoter of a rock festival in Kickapoo Creek, Illinois, was convicted of criminal contempt of court for staging a festival; an appeals court judge upheld a restraining order against the Mountaindale, New York, Festival; ditto, Walpach Township, New Jersey; ditto, Wadena, Iowa; ditto, Powder Ridge, Connecticut; Governor Raymond Shafer of Pennsylvania directed his attorney general to assist the City of Philadelphia in appealing a United States Federal District Court's overruling the City's attempt to prohibit a rock festival; Mayor Kevin H. White of Boston refused to issue a license to Boston College for a three-day rock festival because he couldn't guarantee sufficient police protection.

Perhaps the most unusual manifestation of this trend occurred in Tumer Falls Park, Oklahoma, where Governor Bartlett, the

National Guard, a district judge, and local police all managed to stifle a public rock concert. Even after the promoters had conceded defeat, the harassment persisted. The promoters, who also owned land in the area, invited some 150 people to attend a private rock festival on their grounds. But the local gendarmerie were not to be denied. They were there too, welcoming the guests with road-fitness tests for all cars about to enter the premises.

Another type of local government anarchy is related to the attempts of some petty burghers to expel certain G.I.'s from their midst. Be rude to American soldiers? Yes, but only certain ones.

This type of conspiracy concerns off-base G.I. coffee houses that sprouted near some American Army bases in the late sixties. Case in point: a retreat (in a town we'll call Old Sod) near Fort Knox, Kentucky.

In this case the first step was taken by someone out of government. The landlord of the leasehold decided he'd rather go rentless than let those "Communists" stay on his premises. So, in cahoots with his lawyer (who happened to be the county attorney), he ignored the monthly rent check. Shortly thereafter, the landlord and his attorney went to the County Court and claimed the rent was overdue. The judge duly held that to be so. When the attorney for the coffee house group announced his intention to appeal, the plot thickened.

The next step was taken by the county judge, who immediately set a three-thousand-dollar traverse bond. What is a traverse bond? Under Kentucky law, such a bond guarantees a landlord three months' rent should the tenant's appeal fail. The assumption is that the appeal should take less than that time. But the coffeehouse was paying $250 per month, and a three-thousand-dollar bond assured the landlord twelve months' rent. But even before that money could be raised, the judge looked more thoroughly into the matter and raised the ante to ten thousand dollars! One must conclude that the judge expected the appeal to take at least three and a half years, which would have been slow even in New York City.

The next step was taken by the Old Sod Town Council. It legislated a new business licensing act. Needless to say, on the basis of the new provisions, the coffee house was denied a business license. Furthermore, the Kentucky Health Department "objected to sanitary conditions in the coffee house." Thus, no health permit was issued. On top of this, the chief of police decided that the coffee house was a "nuisance." And, finally, a base spokesman at Fort Knox admitted that there had been "some Army cooperation" in the town's proceedings regarding its most notorious establishment.

The *coup de grâce* was yet to come, and when it did it dried up the coffee house for good. "Then came the arrests. The Meade County Grand Jury subpoenaed and questioned six of the coffee house organizers—and indicted them under the public nuisance and sanitation laws." [2]

So it went, step by step, act by act. Was there a local conspiracy to pass and administer laws harshly in order to accomplish a common political goal? Remember that the United States Constitution forbids the passage of general laws that are a disguise for singling out specific people (bills of attainder). It is also important to remember that, according to the United States government's definition of conspiracy, conspirators are not required to meet or consciously plan any strategy. It is necessary only to prove that the suspects each tried to accomplish the same illegal act in more or less the same time and place. And it is still illegal, under the American system of government, for officials to deny citizens equal protection of the law.

THE GREAT CHICAGO BEFOREMATH

One of the best examples of how a conspiracy to abuse the law may be generated and executed by big-city officials came in Chicago, of all places, prior to the 1968 Democratic National Party Convention. What happened there in April 1968 would probably have escaped national attention had not the tremendous violence erupted in August of that year.

After the Chicago convention riot, several commissions were established to evaluate competing charges of incitement, violence, etc. One such study group, called the Chicago Citizens Commission to Study the Disorders of Convention Week, was staffed by prominent educators, professionals, and clergy. It was chaired by Dr. Edward Sparling, former president of Roosevelt University, Chicago, and the indictment handed down by that group became known as the Sparling Report.

The Sparling Report began by examining, among other things, the past actions of the City of Chicago in issuing street and park permits to political groups, with particular emphasis on unpopular ones. One section of the report discussed the obstacles faced by some of the people who tried to make arrangements for the peace demonstrations of April 27, 1968. The story emerged as follows:

In December 1967, the National Mobilization Committee to End the War in Vietnam (Mobe) scheduled a nationwide ten-day protest. Upon request by National Mobe, the Chicago Peace Council (CPC) agreed to coordinate the relevant events in Chicago, to be climaxed by a massive parade on April 27. The chief coordinator for CPC, Charles Clark Kissinger, began almost immediately to plan the program and negotiate with the responsible local authorities.

In late February, he applied to the Chicago Park District for permission to use the shell in Grant Park. The initial response from the acting superintendent of parks was that the shell was not available; that is, CPC was told that the facility was boarded up and the necessary equipment was in mothballs. Kissinger, unconvinced, took a personal look at the shell and found that only part of it was boarded up. He then told the acting superintendent that CPC would accept the shell as it was and would provide its own equipment. So much for round one.

The superintendent himself requested supplemental information, which included a demand that CPC furnish proof of a three-hundred-thousand-dollar public liability policy and a half-million-dollar performance bond. Kissinger sped back the required information but argued that the financial security provisions were unreasonable. For his trouble, Kissinger was told that no permit would be forthcoming. The reason? "The Chicago Park District is chartered by the State of Illinois for recreational purposes and the use which you request is not in keeping with the dictates of the charter."

Could this mean that the Park District had a general policy against using its facilities for political rallies? If so, then Kissinger could have no quarrel with the superintendent. But the Sparling Report noted, "In June, 1967, permission to use the bandshell had been granted for a Solidarity-with-Israel rally." That sounded somewhat political. The report further noted that "the Park District had granted permission on one day's notice to the Southern Christian Leadership Conference for use of the boarded-up bandshell on April 11, 1968, for a memorial rally to Martin Luther King, Jr.," Neither of these two rallies was simply "recreation." That is fairly certain evidence that the CPC application denial was discriminatory, and therefore illegal.

Shortly thereafter, William L. McFetridge, president of the Park District, publicly commented that the reason for the denial of the Grant Park permit to CPC was "part of a new policy designed to keep unpatriotic groups and race agitators from using park facilities." Chicago was no place to politic or even have fun if local officials decided you were unpatriotic. Unquestionably, the new unofficial regulation was unconstitutionally vague and patently illegal.

Concerning a parade permit, the City of Chicago does not allow two parades in the downtown area on the same day.

That's sane enough. As it happened, April 27 had been reserved for another group prior to the CPC application. Kissinger wrote to the official in charge, James Fitzpatrick, on April 17, and told him, "Virtually any alternative route is acceptable to our organization, and we welcome your suggestions." Kissinger also noted that the anti-Vietnam march could wait until the other parade was over before it would proceed. The Sparling Report noted tersely that this "difficulty was not resolved until April 25" (two days before the parade was scheduled).

Kissinger wanted the parade to terminate at the Civic Center Plaza, where the massed assembly could enjoy a rousing finale, including a battery of speeches. Since the Center was public property, Kissinger did not apply for its use. However, he did inform the management of the Center how they were going to use it on the twenty-seventh. He received a response requesting that he attend a meeting with some city officials. Subsequently he was told by letter that the Center Plaza could not be used on that date because such a large group might obstruct repairs in progress. But the Sparling Committee also noted that Mayor Daley's "Singout for People" Concert was scheduled for the Plaza on April 20 and that twenty-eight motorcycles and operators were permitted to assemble there on April 28 for publicity photographs.

The reader who believes that the CPC had arrived at an impasse is far more cynical than skeptical. For in America compromise is king. The compromise that emerged in Chicago was a model of the art. Among some of the more notable aspects were the following: (1) the District agreed to furnish the sound equipment; (2) a parade permit was issued, but only if the marchers agreed to be "pedestrians," that is, to walk on the sidewalks under police supervision, observing all traffic regulations; (3) the marchers could not occupy the Plaza, but could circle it, and the featured speaker could make an announcement of a special dedication for the Plaza (but not a speech).

But verbal compromises sometimes fail in reality, and it was to be so in Chicago that April. When the demonstrators arrived at the shell, there was no sound equipment whatsoever. "Not our fault," said the city officials. "It was the union. They didn't like your politics, so they refused to bring the equipment." That's not a direct quote, but it was the message.

A small amplification set was found and set up which, according to the Sparling Report, "reached but a small fraction of the crowd." Since few could hear well, it became impossible to tell the crowd about all the nuances to the fragile compromises that had been pieced together, including the complicated orders for the march to and around the Plaza. Mass confusion ensued, with inevitable violations of the compromise. The police waded in and perpetrated some extraordinarily gross acts of violence on the innocent marchers. After all, the demonstrators had broken their word.

Was it unfair for the Sparling Commission to conclude, among other things, that there had been "a concerted effort by city agencies and the Park District to prevent the parade or to destroy its effectiveness?" [3] It seems pretty safe to conclude that this evidence supports a strong suspicion that there was a conspiracy among Chicago administrators as local officials to make the success of the parade as unlikely as possible.

Of course there were rules that could have been interpreted as they were, and there were problems that could have prevented the events as planned, and there were old rusty rules that suddenly popped up and they *were* law.

But the argument that the clearly discriminatory handling of these rules in the case in question amounts to conspiracy is not the same argument that because a policeman stops one speeder out of twelve, he had malice toward that one driver. In heavy traffic, a policeman may have to stop the last of the speeders and let others go. Or an agency may choose to deny a license to more flagrant violators of its regulations as a warning to others who are likely to imitate them. The agency may be overloaded with work and understaffed. There is no *prima facie* case for malice in either of those instances.

In the prelude to April 1968 in Chicago, there was a mass of decisions, all adverse and harassing, all heaping difficulty upon difficulty on a disfavored political group. There was no evidence of extraordinary circumstances (heavy traffic or overworked staff, for example). The pattern of behavior raises a serious question of intent to do harm by a large collection of public administrators, acting as local officials—in concert with local elected officials.

The Sparling Report strongly implies such an intent in its statement that "there is incontrovertible evidence of complications and delays in the issuance of permits to unpopular groups." [4] It is a strong statement that there was an official conspiracy to deprive many American citizens of their equal protection of their law—which is, of course, government anarchy.

THE LITTLE CHICAGO AFTERMATH

There were several private opposition groups itching to impede, mimic, and ridicule the formal rites of the Democratic National Convention in Chicago in August 1968. One was the Coalition for an Open Convention (COC), the establishment antiestablishment contingent of McCarthyites and Kennedyites who wanted to "work within the system." Their major project was to sponsor a massive rally in Soldier Field.

Then there was the Mobe, the unraveled confederation of anti-Vietnamniks, ranging from acid Communist fronts to placid Quakers. Their projected program included mass meetings, parades, and the like.

Finally, there were the Yippies, who try to defy verbal description. The Yippies combine guerrilla theater and guerrilla life. Their intent is to put off the establishment by putting them on. They advocate an end to discourse and a beginning of life. Their politics are not to be taken seriously, but when taken lightly, they become a serious threat to politics. In other words, the Yippies have always been astute enough to achieve their chief goal: media notice.

All three, of course, had to apply to the same Chicago agencies and officials as did CPC that April. They, too, met what the Sparling Report called "a uniform and insistent no."

Before I launch into detail about the actions of Chicago city government before the convention, it would seem to be a good idea to review the laws that at least theoretically should have guided the actions of Chicago administrators and elected officials on the issuance of permits, etc., for political purposes.

Briefly, in the American system there are no absolute rights to speech, assembly, or dissent. The Supreme Court has so stated in numerous decisions over the years. One may disagree with that viewpoint, but it is the stated and currently accepted law of the land, reservations notwithstanding. The Court has seen fit to qualify these freedoms by noting that there may be competing rights that must be given equal, if not greater, weight.

Thus, for example, people cannot parade at will or occupy a city park, since others may want to use that park for their purposes, and many others will probably be trafficking the streets. The Court has also ruled it reasonable for a city to require that groups obtain permits before parading (an exercise of freedom of assembly). The city can also deny such a permit in respect to these other competing needs, but not on the basis of the substantive or ideological merit (or demerit) of the political cause being aired. Such power would be political control over opposing viewpoints—in other words, censorship.

Sometimes the line is hard to draw. Was the official reason for denying a permit the real reason? Or was it a cover for official distaste for the political views of the people applying for the permit? It boils down to a question of patterns: Do the actions and decisions add up to a reasonable suspicion that there was an official conspiracy in Chicago?

Let's take the experience of the Coalition for an Open Convention—the "good Democrats" and "loyal Americans." Their troubles began with their first letter to Mr. Barry, acting superintendent of Chicago's parks. Martin Slate, the COC program director, sent a letter to Barry on July 13 communicating their plans. That was followed by a series of telephone calls spanning nearly two weeks. There was no response.

On July 25, Slate sent a registered letter to Barry and also wrote to Governor Samuel Shapiro. The governor responded two weeks later (by which time it was already August), telling Slate to contact the mayor's office. Finally, on July 29, the superintendent called COC and arrangade a meeting for July 31. The following is COC's view of what happened on that Wednesday, July 31.

> Slate reported that the meeting had been cordial and that Barry had pledged to bring the Coalition's request for facilities before the Park District Commission on Friday, August 2nd. Barry promised at least a tentative decision on a specific site would be reached at that time, and that he would call Slate at 2 P.M. on Friday with that decision. . . . August 2nd Barry failed to call Slate at 2 P.M. as promised. At 2:15 Slate called Barry's office and was told that Barry was "too busy." Barry's secretary said he would return Slate's call. At 4:45 Slate called Barry's office and was told that Barry was gone for the day, to attend the All-Star/Packers game.[5]

It got worse. On August 8, with still no word from the overplayed park superintendent, Slate was informed that the District Board had finally held its meeting, but unfortunately it had not yet acted on the COC requests. The graffiti was on the wall: COC knew it had to resort to legal channels to compel the superintendent to issue the permit.

The Sparling Report had this to say:

> Although the Coalition for an Open Convention presented no threat to either the city or the Democratic Convention, the Chicago Park District and other city officials refused to issue

186

permits, offer alternatives, or even negotiate . . . there is no doubt that the Coalition was denied the basic First Amendment freedoms.

As for the Yippies, let me quote an article from the *Chicago Daily News*, March 26, 1968:

> Park District officials, when met by the Yippie delegation dressed in long hair, togas, beads, white makeup and such, told the Yippies, "You know there's a law against sleeping in the park all night." Responded the Yippies, "We don't plan to sleep all night. We plan to make love all night." Park officials, after calling attention to the need for formal requests and provision for insurance, referred the Yippies to City Hall.

Now, the Yippies had neither spleen nor stomach to fight City Hall. But they did perform theater for the troops of Chicago officialdom, hoping to taunt them into acting illegally. They were eminently successful, given the willingness of their "audience" to comply and, not surprisingly, the Yippies, too, decided to go to court. (As we all learned, Abbie Hoffman figured the courts would be the finest way to get the establishment to pervert its own values in a theatrically dramatic fashion.)

Mobe, because it had developed the most comprehensive set of plans, had to deal with the largest number of Chicago officials. Once again, it had to be determined whether the Park District would allow people to assemble in the city's park. And once again, it had to be learned whether the Bureau of the Streets would permit unpopular political traffic.

The parade charade began early, on June 16. Aside from the usual problems that the City raised concerning parks and parades, a new element was introduced—the parade route. City officials claimed to worry over the potential for violence if the marchers tried to proceed through certain specified avenues near the convention site (the Amphitheatre). These areas were known to house regiments of bigots, all drooling at the chance to welcome the demonstrators.

It should perhaps be noted that in a system of government

like that in America, where there are so many levels of government, one government agency or level sometimes acts contrary to the interests or plans of another. And so it was here. The United States Justice Department was headed at the time by Ramsey Clark, who feared that the city of Chicago was launched on a collision course with the new army of protestants. Through its Community Relations Service, the Department of Justice therefore tried to constitute itself as mediator between the Daley administration and some members of the demonstration leadership.

According to the Sparling Commission, "Justice Department officials concluded that the Mayor was not interested in negotiating a compromise." The Department also believed the City would almost certainly deny all the permits, and it tried to persuade the demonstration leadership of this early in August. But the demonstration efforts continued. Finally, at a meeting between some of the demonstration leaders and Deputy Mayor Robert Stahl (on August 10), the organizers were informed that Mayor Daley did not issue permits; only the agencies were responsible for that. That was certainly not news to Mobe. And time was running out.

Mobe made one last try at making favorable contact with the city bureaucracy on August 12. Separate telegrams were sent to the Park District, the Department of Streets and Sanitation, and the Police Department.

Essentially, the telegram invited responsible officials to meet with the Mobe National leadership, who were arriving in Chicago to work out final plans. None of the officials showed up, although Stahl, Assistant Corporation Counsel Elrod, and an official from the Youth Welfare Commission were there. But Stahl had already informed the Mobe of his own impotence on these matters, and the other two officials could be no more virile. Mobe heaved a collective sigh.

When the Park District finally met on August 13, they managed to overlook Mobe's application. Undoubtedly they were too busy again. A last-ditch telegram was dispatched to Daley urging him to attend an emergency meeting. What happened? No show. The demonstration steering committee met shortly thereafter and decided to go to court.

Assuming that the Sparling Commission was correct in its account of the facts, its interpretation of these facts seems to be the conclusion a reasonable man would reach.

> For public places covered by an ordinance or permit mechanism, no criteria exist to narrow the discretion of licensing officials. Furthermore, at every stage in the licensing procedure, the burden of initiative was placed upon those citizens seeking a permit. As a result, there was no means of compelling a prompt disposition of a request either administratively or through the courts.[6]

In other words, even where the officials were clearly—and illegitimately—impeding and delaying a legitimate request, there was nothing that could be done within the system. Furthermore,

> In actual operation these ordinances were so administered as constantly to deny equal protection of the law. Some groups have been readily permitted to parade; others have been strangled in red tape.[7]

In other words, the Chicago administration was guilty of official malfeasance. It was official anarchy pure and simple, yet nothing could be done about it. Who, then, was proximately responsible for the bloodshed in the streets? And to what extent were the Chicago police themselves victims of a higher government anarchy?

INSURRECTION RESURRECTION

All these examples are rank amateurism compared to the tough fabric of official anarchy woven into attempts by Southern officials at all levels to evade and defy the Supreme Court of the United States since 1954. This was hardly the first outbreak of Southern rebellion since the Civil War, but this time the camouflage was discarded, and the real nature of continuing insurrection exposed.

Actually, being a "rebel" has always been *au courant* in America's Southland. The Stars and Bars, and Confederate-type uniforms, have been Southern high school symbols ever since Lee's sword was turned into a plowshare. The rebel yell still remains as modish in Georgia as the Dixie cup. And Ole Miss's teams, always a crunching football power, still call themselves "The Rebels." And against whom is all this hostile élan focused? The national government, the permanent personification of George III. Of course, this happens when the federal government is shackling Southern officials from freely desecrating the Bill of Rights, not when it is showering Southern citizens with soothing subsidies.

"Insurrection" might be a bad word to describe what has been happening in the South regularly and widely since the mid-fifties. But it is even more accurate than anarchy. Insurrections, like revolutions, are almost always organized and led. Official anarchy, as a more often than sometimes thing, just happens. But even where it happens widely, it usually lacks leadership. Leadership in the second Southern insurrection, with which other Americans have had to contend openly, has come mainly from elected officials: governors, mayors, U.S. representatives, U.S. senators, judges state and federal, and state legislators.

What makes this anarchy, though, as far as the South is concerned, is that despite the breakdown of a substantial part of the American legal system, there has been no systematically organized movement throughout the entire Southland. The way official anarchy has been practiced in the South is a tribute to the practical genius of men who feel their backs against the wall. The power of hostile superlaw can be most frightening to those who are pledged to support it.

Back in 1962, James Meredith was trying to enter the University of Mississippi as its first black student. Twists and turns of the legal process kept him out for a long time. But the legal process in America, though cumbersome, is still not totally incapable of dealing with a case like Meredith's, and time finally ran out for Ole Miss.

In late September 1962, the courts ordered Meredith admitted to the university. Governor Ross Barnett was found in contempt of court for meddling with Meredith's admission to the university (a charge for which the governor received no punishment), and on September 30 and October 1, all hell broke loose in Oxford, Mississippi. President John F. Kennedy ordered federal troops to quell the large-scale violence. Facing what has been so often the Southern dilemma, Southern officials felt called upon to drum up justification for what had been done; they had to show (at least to themselves) that their interference with declared law was legally justified. They claimed they were not outside the law; it was the law that was illegitimate.

Later in October, the Mississippi Junior Chamber of Commerce published a short pamphlet entitled *Oxford: A Warning for Americans,* which tried to prove the illegal nature of the federal government's position at Ole Miss and the legality of the actions of Mississippi officials. Shortly thereafter, another pamphlet appeared: a reprint of a speech by a past president of the American Bar Association—who was also a White Citizens Council leader and a close associate of Governor Barnett. The arguments in these pamphlets demonstrated even more clearly how illegally the Mississippi power elite did act.

Their first contention was that the ancient doctrine of interposition, completely discredited by all American courts and all reputable scholars, held. It is, simply, the assertion that a state can interpose its own concept of law and justice between its citizens and the federal government. This doctrine leaves America with no solid union at all. It was settled once by the Southern defeat in the Civil War. To raise it again was to raise a cry for more civil war, which was nothing less than a call to treason.

Another major argument was that the Fourteenth Amendment itself was invalid. By taking this stance, men who had sworn to uphold the Constitution denied its very existence. These were men who knew that courts decide such matters, and that courts long ago decided it was valid. They also knew the Fourteenth Amendment was an integral part of the American system.

An even more pathetic attempt to create a legal guise for illegal action was the allegation that the decision in *Brown v. Board of Education* was not "the law of the land." They argued that *Brown* applied only to the specific case involving the city of Topeka, Kansas, and not to every board of education in the country. The authors and advocates of these pamphlets were men schooled and trained in the Anglo-American common law system, and the essence of that common law system is that cases decided by courts of highest jurisdiction become binding for all similar cases. High court cases, in America, are generally, not specially, applicable. A decision that involved one school board was meant to apply, and did apply, to all school boards in America. Yet this argument, made by a former president of the American Bar Association, was used to justify local official actions against highest court judgments.

In order to repudiate the contempt-of-court citation against Governor Barnett, the pamphlets argued that the governor was illegally convicted since he was not present at the hearing. What they failed to mention was that Governor Barnett was notified of the proceedings and personally refused to appear as ordered. His absence could not absolve him from the consequences of the trial.

But the main grievance in these Southern position papers was the calling in of the National Guard. Once again a convoluted interpretation of the United States Constitution provided the major theme. As in most interpretations of gospel, one part of the revered document was miscited and more relevant portions were overlooked.

The pamphlets noted that Article II expresses the uninfringeable right of a state to maintain a militia. But what is the relevance of this provision to what happened? It is oblique at best. In fact, the state militia (the National Guard) had been used. The regular U.S. Army was not sent to Mississippi. Moreover, it was not even the entire National Guard (of the state) that had been utilized, so the state was still maintaining its militia.

The U.S. Constitution does specifically provide, however, that the militia may be called in order to "execute the laws of the Union" and to "suppress insurrection." This is a lot clearer in applicability than other cited provisions, but it goes unnoticed, uncited, and unloved. Furthermore, it is the President who has had the power, historically, to make the judgment as to when to call out troops. Indeed, in 1895, after the President had used federal troops to suppress a railway strike, the Supreme Court stated unequivocally, "If the emergency arises, the army of the Nation, and all its militia, are at the service of the Nation to compel obedience to its laws." [8]

So much for the false legal coloration to the new insurrection. How wide and how deep was it and is it in the South? It spans the entire Southern political spectrum. All kinds of leaders have been involved; all types of bureaucrats. The names of several Southern governors became household words simply by their proclaiming their defiance of the law they vowed to defend. Orville Faubus, for instance—the name lingers, the man doesn't. Ross Barnett. What can anyone remember about him other than his explicit recantation of national law and order? Only George Wallace rose from illicit local acts of prominence to genuine national stature. This occurred by his championing of national movements readily identifiable with Southern resistance, and by transforming numbers into political power through the anachronism for the electoral college.

A perfect example of the flamboyance with which this illegality is still enjoyed by Southern governors was the recent case of Governor Kirk's contempt of court. Southern resistance to school desegregation was dealt a paralyzing blow in 1970, at least legally and formally. The finishing political touch was ostensibly performed by the Department of Justice under the direction of President Richard M. Nixon. Dutifully, lower federal courts throughout the South made the requisite commands to diehard school districts to desegregate.

Some officials, however, like Kirk, decided to take a last plunge into official anarchy. Not only did Kirk advise students and teachers in the school district of Manatee to ignore the courts' orders; he also assumed "custodial supervision" of the school system. Why did he do it? According to the governor, it was strictly in "the best interest of the children." [9]

The governor was not content to do this quietly, from the sanctity and remoteness of his gubernatorial quarters. He broke upon the scene, directing every participant in this conspiracy to insult the law of the land. In this particular scenario, the governor was joined by the lieutenant governor of the state and two assistant superintendents of the school district.

The rather conspicuous absence of the superintendent (the official normally in charge) was due to the fact that Kirk had purged the post in order to assume its duties himself. Whatever reasons lay behind his action, the governor was as contumacious of court as any judge-vilifying Black Panther—and so were the officials of the school district in league with him. Even the Department of Justice, uncharacteristically casting verbal caution asunder, blasted Kirk, saying it was "inadmissible that any officer—high or low—would assume the stance that he will not obey the order of any court. . . ." [10]

Actually, the whole affair between Kirk, his associates, the courts, and the federal government was a sham. Almost immediately after the court order, its provisions were carried out; i.e., the busing began and the school classrooms were integrated. The saddest part of all is that Kirk could believe in the local political value of his proclamation of lawbreaking. Hopefully, his subsequent defeat for reelection was related to his official anarchy.

One catalog of Southern official lawlessness is a legal anthology published in 1965, edited by Leon Friedman, called *Southern Justice*.[11] It includes nineteen articles written by lawyers, some of the "outside agitators" who migrated southward for 1964's summer of political frolic. Most of the lawyers were sponsored by the Lawyers Constitutional Defense Committee (LCDC), and all the sordid stories and dismal details are the accounts of these men.

Item:

A group of young civil rights workers founded a "Freedom School" and a community center and were well into the process of helping Negro voters register. One afternoon, a white member of the group stopped by a black high school to watch football practice, and he began to talk with some of the students there. He was arrested on charges including trespass and inciting to riot.

When the police realized they couldn't make the charges stick, a meeting followed between the mayor of the town, the chief of police, and a lawyer from LCDC. The mayor told the lawyer that the freedom workers could not remain in the town after dark; if they did, they would be arrested. There would be no charge against them, they would simply be detained for their own good. It was called "protective custody." When the lawyer protested, he was told he could lodge no complaint until after their arrest. The boys would be released about 4 A.M.— an unusually unsafe time for civil libertarians to roam around Southern boulevards.

The civil rights workers refused to be intimidated by this thinly veiled threat and arranged to visit with a Negro family the next evening. The mayor called a special meeting, and, along with the aldermen, passed a resolution that "all civil rights workers in the City . . . at the close of the normal working day shall be taken into protective custody and held in the City Jail until the beginning of the next normal working day of the police force." [12]

This was done, the boys were arrested, and a lengthy and costly legal action had to be instituted.

Item:

The Louisiana Criminal Code, Title 14, Article 103, read (in 1964) as follows: "Disturbing the peace is the doing of any of the following in such a manner as would foreseeably disturb or alarm the public: . . . (7) Commission of any other act in such a manner as to unreasonably disturb or alarm the public."

In Garner, Louisiana, in 1960, several college students "sitting in" were arrested for violating section 7, above. According to the police and the prosecutor, the public was alarmed by their activity. A long, tortuous journey through the federal courts began, ending in the Supreme Court of the United States. The Court declared the convictions null and void. Obviously, the lawful action of some students, even if alarming to segments of the population, could not justify a prosecution and conviction, much less an arrest. But the decision of the Supreme Court did not spell finish to section 7 in the sovereign state of Louisiana.

Several years later, two white voter registration workers were apprehended under the provisions of section 7—because their activities alarmed the people of West Monroe, Louisiana. It was also against the law for anyone to walk down the streets of West Monroe with someone of another race during the voter registration drive—because it alarmed the people of West Monroe, Louisiana. Peter Teachout, a Harvard Law student on duty there, tells us that a city attorney in West Monroe stated that the Supreme Court may have decided the law of the land in the Garner case, but "they haven't declared it unconstitutional up here yet."

Item:

Several methods have been used to illegally deny Negroes their constitutional right to vote in the American South.

The *U.S. Commission on Civil Rights Report No. 1 on Voting* (1961) is an authoritative source on the degree and methodology of official illegality in depriving Southern blacks of their right to ballot. Some of their findings were as follows:

1. There are reasonable grounds to believe that substantial numbers of Negro citizens are, or recently have been, denied the right to vote on grounds of race or color in about 100 counties in eight Southern States: Alabama, Florida, Georgia, Louisiana, Mississippi, North Carolina, South Carolina, and Tennessee. Some denials of the right to vote occur by reason of discriminatory application of laws setting qualifications for voters. Other denials result from arbitrary and discriminatory procedures for the registration of voters; still others occur by reason of threats and intimidation, or the fear of retaliation.

2. Some States have given encouragement to such discriminatory denials of the right to vote. The Legislature of Louisiana, for instance, has fostered discrimination against Negro voters by the enactment of restrictive voter qualification laws and by the activities of its voter qualification laws in such fashion as to permit, if not encourage, discrimination against the would-be Negro voter. The Alabama Legislature has tried unsuccessfully to eliminate Negro voters from the city of Tuskegee. . . .

11. The right to vote is denied in some places not only by the discriminatory application of legal qualifications for voters . . . but in addition by the arbitrary or discriminatory application of various registration procedures, such as the following:

(a) The requirement of a specified number of registered voters as "vouchers" to identify would-be voters. This practice is particularly effective in disfranchising Negroes when there are no Negroes already registered, and no whites will "vouch" for Negroes; or where a rule is enforced limiting the number of times a given voter may "vouch" for another.

(b) The imposition of other unduly technical requirements for identification of would-be voters.

(c) The rejection of applicants for registration, or the re-

197

moval of voters from the rolls, on grounds of minor technical errors in the completion of required forms.

(d) Refusing or failing to notify registrants whether or not they have been registered.

(e) Imposing various forms of delay in the registration process.

Most Southern voting requirements included a test of the applicants' ability to interpret properly the state constitution. A registrar administered the test. Needless to say, whites usually fared better. The problem was that far more rigorous standards were applied to Negro applicants. "In one instance 'FRDUM FOOF SPETCH' was an acceptable response to the request to interpret Article 1, section 3 of the Louisiana Constitution" [13] on a white man's application. But the literacy test devastated the ranks of potential Negro voters: "In November, 1962, the state carried 37,365 illiterates on the registration rolls. One registrar flunked eight Negro school teachers while passing eight illiterate white ones." [14]

Instances and statistics like these led Judge Wisdom of the Fifth Circuit Court of Appeals to find in 1963 that there was "massive policy in a pattern based on the regular, consistent, predictable, unequal application of the test." [15]

Erwin Griswold, the Solicitor General of the United States in 1971, noted that "Negroes could not find the registrars though white persons had no difficulty . . . registrars would reject applications because they said there were 'mistakes' in them. In one case . . . the 'mistake' was that the applicant had underlined the word 'Mr.' on the card instead of circling it. . . ." [16]

Once the evidence of voting discrimination has been brought into court, the courts usually reverse the process and the Negro voter gets his opportunity to register. The major difficulty is getting it that far. Knowing this has given Southern officials, including legislators, another point at which to break the law in collusion with one another. For example, one section of the Civil Rights Act of 1960 makes it mandatory for local officials to yield records in their custody when they are requested by the Attorney General of the United States. All well and good. But there are all sorts of questions and problems that might crop up in response to this simple federal mandate. And they usually do.

Case in point: A county registrar was directed to turn over the voting records. He refused, saying that the records were not in his custody. He had turned them over to the grand jury. Did he use them? Yes, on a daily basis. But they were physically in the possession of the grand jury.

Another case: Local officials interpreted the request for records as tantamount to a criminal prosecution. They therefore demanded that the request be absolutely precise. It took two years for the courts to decide that this was not what that section of the Civil Rights Act was all about.

Moreover, that title of the Civil Rights Act specifically directed "every officer of election [to] retain and preserve . . . all records and papers which come into his possession relating to any application, registration. . . ." As Professor Donald Strong of the University of Alabama observed, "Congress has specified what papers must be preserved. Hence, there can be no room for a quibble about what papers are to be made available. . . ." [17] Small wonder that one law professor suggested that the confrontation at Selma, Alabama, in 1964, was more likely caused by "official disobedience" than by "civil disobedience." [18]

Item:

One day, two white student workers received a brutal physical mugging at the hands of a gasoline station owner. They decided to press charges against him.

The usual practice when someone is a complaining witness in a criminal case is that the prosecuting attorney keeps him fully apprised of trial dates. This was not done. The witnesses had to persist to learn when and where the trial was to be held. On the scheduled date for trial, they both went to the courthouse at the proper time, where they were told that the trial had been adjourned for a week. The defendant was not to be seen—probably because he had been told. The two complaining witnesses were given no account of why the trial had been postponed.

The two witnesses reappeared in court a week later. Apparently the acting city attorney was handling cases that day. He thumbed through the docket with the two men and their attorney and discovered that the case was not even listed for trial. A scouring of the whole docket for all cases scheduled for trial regardless of date revealed that the case had disappeared. The acting city attorney looked flabbergasted. He suggested that the two witnesses and their lawyer approach the city attorney when he returned from the state capital the next day, which they did.

The city attorney looked just as baffled as his acting counterpart. He said he couldn't understand what had happened to the case either. When asked whether he could set the case for the next day, he replied that he could not. In fact, he couldn't be ready for trial until the following Monday. Strange. He should have been prepared the day before. Not so strange, for the summer was almost over and the students had to return North at the end of the week. Without the presence of the complaining witnesses, there would be no trial.

Jesse Brenner, a New York attorney at the time, and the legal counsel for the two boys, was a bit skeptical about the chances of the cases really being tried the following Monday. "The city attorney," he speculated, "would continually misplace the case, be out of town or invent some other excuse until Mike and Don were gone. What depressed me so about Mississippi's make-believe world of justice was that this conversation with a city attorney was typical of like conversations anywhere." [19]

Item:

During the picketing of some stores, twenty-odd Negro college students were arrested. At a mass meeting on the campus of

Southern University that night, an announcement was made of a demonstration in front of the courthouse in Baton Rouge to protest the jailing of the students. One of the leaders of the march informed the police chief that the group was going to the courthouse to make their feelings known through patriotic songs and prayers. The chief told the leader to keep his group across from the courthouse—which he did.

As the demonstration progressed, a crowd of 150 whites gathered on the courthouse steps. There were some eighty to ninety policemen on hand, too. When the prisoners joined the protest singing from the jailhouse, the demonstrators were ordered to move out. They didn't. Gas followed, and then the police. Many arrests were made, including that of the leader.

Among the charges brought against the leader was "obstructing justice": some judges and jurors had apparently avoided the courthouse because of the furor. The leader was convicted.

Some time later, the Supreme Court of the United States saw fit to reverse this conviction, observing that the state could not try a demonstrator for obstructing justice when he did only that which he had been given permission to do by the police. But that was obvious; the police had led the whole group into an ambush, an intentional plan to lure the group into a situation where there could be some pretense to throw them into jail too.[20]

Item:

Miss Mary Hamilton went on the witness stand in the circuit court of Etowah County, Alabama, to testify on her own *habeas corpus* petition. She was in jail because of her participation in a civil rights demonstration. The following colloquy ensued:

> *Cross Examination by Solicitor Rayburn:*
> Q. What is your name, please?
> A. Miss Mary Hamilton.
> Q. Mary, I believe—you were arrested—who were you arrested by?
> A. My name is Miss Hamilton. Please address me correctly.

Q. Who were you arrested by, Mary?

A. I will not answer a question—

By Attorney Amaker: The witness' name is Miss Hamilton.

A. —your question until I am addressed correctly.

THE COURT: Answer the question.

THE WITNESS: I will not answer them unless I am addressed correctly.

THE COURT: You are in contempt of court.[21]

The Supreme Court of Alabama upheld the contempt of court citation, stating among other things that the petitioner's name was Mary Hamilton, not Miss Mary Hamilton. But everyone knows that by Southern tradition, white women are called Miss, and black women are addressed by their first names. This is common practice in most Southern courtrooms as well.

Once again, it took the Supreme Court of the United States to make judicial use of this fact and quash that judgment. As the Supreme Court of the United States saw it, it was courtroom segregation, countenanced and practiced by prosecutors, with positive reinforcement by judges, through all the trial and appellate courts of the state.[22]

There is no doubt that the degree of official anarchy in the South is lessening, particularly in matters of educational and electoral desegregation. The tone of Southern politics is becoming much more moderate toward integration policies (witness the gubernatorial elections of 1970), and it seems safe to say that fewer and fewer racial bombasts will occupy high Southern offices in the near future. All of this, however, in no way means that the problems have been completely resolved. The battle for law and order in the South has simply been moving into a new, more sophisticated phase, but it is still defiantly crude around the edges.

Senator Walter Mondale (D-Minn.), in his capacity of chairman of the Senate Committee on Equal Educational Opportunity, took a short tour through Dixie in the summer of 1970. He wanted firsthand information on what he had heard in his committee about a variety of continuing abuses, e.g., classroom segregation after buildings were integrated; selective firing of Negro teachers; increased public fund transference to so-called private academies. When the senator returned, he had a lot to say about what he had seen and heard.

First of all, he noted that all of the above practices were "widespread." [23] Moreover, he stated that "at least in communities I visited, discrimination and repression of minority groups is severe and blatantly open. This ranged from police brutality to insults, to economic sanctions. . . ." [24]

Worse yet—as an indication of federal complicity with the local official anarchy—"person after person told [Mondale] of their efforts to involve the [U.S. Justice] department in protecting their rights, their attempts to report these abuses to the FBI and Justice Department attorneys, and the lack of action or the negative action they received." [25] As recently as April 1971, the Southern Regional Council (what *Newsweek* calls a "liberal biracial research organization") corroborated all these points and termed the phenomenon "re-segregation." [26]

So the Southern local conspiracy thrives and prospers, and will persevere because it has accommodated itself to certain national pressures and gone an inch or so underground. It may not be as frightening as it once was, but it is now more dangerous and more difficult to weed out.

Conspiracy among local officials to rid themselves of those they consider a threat to their values is a particularly dangerous strain of government anarchy. Whether it be north or south of Washington, D.C., it combines the power of many branches of government—eliminating the safety in the separation of powers —and is colored by the healthy glow of respectability. The opposition, whether blacks, students, peace workers, or hippies, is usually low in finances, outstripped in techniques, and dilettantish in its use of the system.

What is worse is that the entire system as presently constituted and staffed is peculiarly unwilling or unable to cope with this kind of anarchy. Many people in power seem crippled when faced by the prospect of criminally prosecuting government anarchists. This is due in large part to the fact that government has become such a huge and persuasive faction itself. So those in government, who might be able to initiate action, just blush or bluster at such charges, or find their hands tied by structural inadequacies in the system. Even those few predisposed to do something about it are as helpless as the victims.

But enough. It is high time we turned from diagnosis to prescription. First, let's take a look at some of the current and projected alternative solutions to the problem of government anarchy.

8

First Aid
Is Little Help

If pain persists for more than
10 days, consult your physician.
—*Bufferin bottle*

As I said at the outset, a lot of people have spent parcels of time figuring out how to alleviate the plague of official anarchy which is debilitating America. Some have even taken steps—aside from the usual friendly commiseration—to do something about it.

STOP THE COPS

It is not ironic that the major focal point of government lawlessness should evoke the most pressure and suggestions for reform. I don't know whether police anarchy is actually more widespread than other forms, but it is the most irritating, probably because it is the most painful. We fear physical pain more than other kinds, and when police act lawlessly it is often physical.

In America, what is ironic is that the police themselves (that is, some top police officials) have more than a passing concern about it all. They know they are the migraine, and they have offered some buffer against themselves, for as professionals they also know that much police lawlessness is, at least, amateurish conduct. It rightly offends their sense of professional pride. Then, too, a good many realize they are American citizens first and local policemen second. The rape of civil liberties, practiced as routine by many members of their own departments, offends them as much as it does some private citizens.

Some people will argue, of course, that police lawlessness is so rare as to be a freak. Others will argue that it is not rare, but believe that it is usually unintentional—a product of vague policies and poor command. Still others will admit that it is often intentional and that it is a serious enough problem to consider drastic remedies in police organization.

These men are policemen, too, and they believe fervently in the importance of safety for their force, as well as its effectiveness and morale. They worry that a purge of a large minority of their men might seriously damage these three goals, perhaps irreparably. And they fear—with some justification—that outside restrictions might also hamper the safety, efficiency, and morale of their departments, and they are extremely wary of them.

We are all in a dilemma. We want change—but all proposals are met by arguments that they may be more dangerous than the problem. When propolice extremists deny that the situation is serious, this counteracts any serious intention to effectuate serious remedies and little is done to actually change the situation. Some half-hearted attempts at reform are made, mainly to "improve" recruitment and to better police relations with the public.

One of the causes of police anarchy inheres in the attitudes of the offending policemen. Some police officials understand this. Their recruitment programs include ways to improve the caliber of policemen; to their way of thinking, a more professional cop will produce a more professional performance.

The major avenues toward this goal are better pay and better fringe benefits, in addition to improved postentrance educational programs. Several police departments are financing college recruitment trips. They report significant success along these lines, mainly because police work can furnish ample intellectual and social satisfaction for many products of the contemporary American college scene. Mayor Frank Fasi of Honolulu came up with an interesting variation: police ROTC on American college campuses.

College recruitment of police would go some of the way toward diminishing police lawlessness. Still, a sizable dent will be made in it only after America has gained a volunteer force of middle-class, college-educated, socially oriented police—which will probably take at least a generation or two. Changing the balance of middle-class/working-class recruits could create other problems, as even liberal police officials acknowledge. Such a police force would probably resent some necessary paramilitary discipline and might also be far too lenient and verbose in situations that call for quick reaction or terminal violence. Furthermore, a majority of college rookies creates a tremendous tradition gap between the veterans and the newcomers: just as the liberal tendencies of many police academies are subverted by field experience, so might college-socialized ideas create tensions with the experience of older cops, at least for a long, long time.

Partly because such programs are still eons away from producing any visible percentage of enlightened and reoriented professional police, and partly because such a resocialization of personnel cannot eliminate whatever police lawlessness inheres in the nature of the job, some police officials still remain open to new ideas for restructuring police work itself. Those with less insight see the solution in terms of "better community relations."

Beginning with the proposition that there is a lack of communication between the police and the community, many police officials become terribly excited over their so-called community relations programs. Chicago, for instance, called its program "Walk and Talk." In New York City, it has been called "PEP"— Preventive Enforcement Patrol. Assistant Chief Inspector Eldridge Waith, commandant of the N.Y.P.D. unit, notes that his outfit performs its community relations while on regular police routine, but that "we want to show the people that we're sensitive to their problems and that we understand the community." [1]

The St. Louis program, one of the first, has employed a civilian director for each district "committee." He would guide but did not "control" the committee. According to Jules Gerard, a professor of law at Washington University, each committee was divided into subcommittees. For instance, "the Juvenile Subcommittee solicits residents to act as 'block watchers'—people who

209

watch the street while children are going to and from school. It also arranges 'cruiser tours' for high school students; students spend an evening riding in unmarked cars answering calls, thus getting a first-hand picture of the life of a patrolman." [2]

Like animal crackers, there is a great, though limited, variety in the species, and these programs may well generate a more acute community sensitivity to the ups and downs of the policeman's daily seesaw. Doubtless, they will help police better understand the community. It is probable, however, that most police are far more concerned with changing their image than with changing their procedures and effectively curbing police lawlessness. Like animal crackers, they offer minimal nourishment to someone who is starving. The concept of "community relations" is much too close for comfort to "public relations." Police lawlessness is real, and PR is mainly talk.

There is another problem that makes both these approaches (better recruitment and community relations) less than satisfactory, if satisfaction is tantamount to a large-scale national decrease in police anarchy. There is a difference between the number of policemen in America and the number of police departments. Much statistical "progress" reported through these police programs is related to the fact that there are now more individual policemen who are more professional and who are involved in community relations programs of one sort or another. In other words, the statistics show a somewhat larger number of professional and socially aware policemen than ever before.

However, there are numerous small police departments around the country which have taken none to few steps toward college recruitment or better community relations—or even in professional training. For instance, in one recent study of a small Midwestern police department (a city of 150,000), police were asked under what circumstances they thought they should use violence. The category which received the largest number of affirmative replies was "disrespect for police." Thirty-seven percent thought that "roughing a man up" was justified. Some

19 percent thought it was also justified "to obtain information." [3]

The degree of police anarchy in smaller cities and townships probably remains at least as high as ever, and the percentage of police departments that are becoming more professional is much smaller than the percentage of policemen. There seems little likelihood that there will be significant professionalization in these middle-fry departments in the foreseeable future, since local communities tend to support policemanship, however crudely it is done ("Support your Local Police"), and there are too few who support reform measures.

Moreover, better schooling and recruiting and better pay and some elbow-rubbing in the ghettoes are not going to dent many metropolitan types of police lawlessness like wide-scale illegal searches and large-scale infiltration. Illegal searches and illegal wiretapping, among other methods, are indispensable to current notions of police efficiency. They also offer tangible benefits to "law enforcement."

Police brutality, on the other hand, does not. Brutality is principally a simple therapy for ailing personalities. Police brutality may be lessened by programs in civilization, college drafting, and public relations, but such programs are unlikely to lessen appreciably the degree of other police-essential kinds of police lawlessness.

Nonpolice pressure, particularly that brought to bear by civilian review boards, causes the police the greatest consternation. A civilian review board is seen by some segments of the citizenry as a checkpoint, staffed mainly by nonpolicemen, who can receive, investigate, and act upon complaints like those discussed previously. It is recommended, usually with fervor, despite the existence of internal boards, staffed solely by police, already operating in most police departments. In fact, the police police the police almost everywhere, but many nonpolice believe they do not do so with as much relish as they police the outside community.

As might be expected, almost all policemen resist external

review efforts and try their utmost to undo them. They are attacked on a broad front. The police are quick to note that nonpolice cannot properly understand difficulties in policing and that their "interference" with proper police law enforcement deeply undermines police morale.

Sometimes, as in New York City, the civilian review board becomes a heated political issue and a pitched political war erupts. The New York City civilian board became an infant mortality through a 1966 referendum. On the other hand, the Police Advisory Board in Philadelphia prospered longer, and there is a sister agency in the District of Columbia. Critics outside civilian review, who claim it damages police efficiency and morale, are forced to refute the fact that Philadelphia ranked lowest in crime rates among America's major cities, even in 1970, when the crime scare reached the level of presidential politics. Furthermore, Police Chief Wilson of the District of Columbia told me he preferred outside review; it saved his force the time and energy it would have to invest in such unpleasant work.

Much can be said for both sides in this dispute: nonpolicemen may well fail to grasp nuances involved in pressing police problems, and the police are clearly too defensive and lax with complaints. For instance, in a recent study of the New York Police Department's handling of complaints against policemen, of 541 complaints made during one period of time, only one case resulted in even a major fine.[4] The study also noted that for charges that police violated *departmental* rules, over 50 percent resulted in some sort of punishment. Internal police review boards have always been too much placebo and all too little nostrum. Suggestions made by an external board arouse so much wrath among police and benevolent associations as to make their utility marginal at best.

But perhaps the police have a special right to be indignant. Too often they alone are singled out, while other agencies at least as guilty of large-scale lawlessness among their employees are rarely put on the spot.

Think back for a moment. We've noted the tremendous amount of anarchy rampant in American prisons, in America's military, among its prosecutors, its welfare agencies, its courts, and elsewhere. Yet there is a near void of internal awareness or outside pressure for these institutions to do anything about it.

What usually happens is that some item of official anarchy, blazing across the national scene for a day or two, will evoke passionate oratory from a few senators or liberal spokesmen. After the initial clutch of "no comments" and a few *ad hominem* counterattacks, official announcement will be made of a suspension or two, a court martial, a shuffling of personnel, or a shifting of responsibility.

For example, when Senator Sam Ervin's committee heard disclosures of domestic snooping by the Army, the immediate consequence was that a few officers faced premature retirement, the responsibility for further internal spying was transferred to the Department of Justice, and Justice officials stated that such internal intelligence was essential and should remain beyond public scrutiny, indeed, even beyond the authority of the courts. In other words, within government there was some discomfort, followed by some fiddling around with personnel and nomenclature, but the situation remained basically the same.

Occasional prison and bureaucratic scandals end similarly. There is a great storm about how extraordinary it all is. This is followed by flurries of activity to "remedy" the immediate source of embarrassment, but little is done to alter the structure comprehensively so that it will not happen again. Oh, there is an occasional "experiment" or two, but one gets the feeling that the more successful they are, the more obscure they will become. It seems to me that America has always been dedicated to patching things up with mercurochrome and bandages. Maybe it is part of the frontier heritage, where one had to make things do. And then, once they seem to work, they become part of tradition, demanding awe-ful respect, even when it is clear that the makeshift has not continued to work so well at all.

A DECLARATION OF DEPENDENCE

The American citizenry permits government lawlessness to recur time and again. It refuses to consider novel, generally applicable measures to stem these steady eruptions of official lawlessness.

Part of the reason—probably a large part—is that most Americans already believe there is a general way to handle this, one that has worked well enough in the past, which includes a syndrome of institutions for investigation and prosecution. The problem-solving starts with study commissions or legislative investigations, moves occasionally through grand juries, and almost inevitably rests upon some mystical reliance on the judiciary.

Reliance on the judiciary is the key to the American faith that government anarchy can be stopped. Study commissions come and go, with all the authority in the world to produce volumes of facts and no power to accomplish anything. Grand juries are the Tom Sawyers of America's check-and-balance machinery: past masters at palming off whitewash jobs on their closest friends, who were interested enough to watch them work.

Americans tend to think of courts when they think of curing the intolerable situations that government creates. For one thing, there are enough judges and lawyers populating the federal, state, and local landscapes to create a sense of some security. When in trouble with government, get a lawyer. If an agency feigns paralysis, or acts illegally, or the military sends a squad of scapegoats up the river, or a particular judge is cockeyed with hate, Americans look to the courts. Some judge or other will eventually take care of it. But will he?

Americans aren't the first to dream about an elite group of supersocialized specialists, sitting in placid isolation, considering how to keep government within bounds. Plato was. At least he was the first to write about it. In *The Laws*, he wrote that democratic rulers would sometimes be too enamored of their own preeminence or of their ability to manipulate the popular vote to abide by the immutable laws of their fundamental governance. He suggested creating a special group of learned and wise men who comprehended a higher and more unified law than mere democratic law, that is, the rule of "virtue."

This clique would convene before the crack of dawn for the purpose of reviewing the actions of government. They were to be called, appropriately, the Nocturnal Council, and though their powers were never detailed by Plato, it would seem that they were to have ultimate power over lesser government functionaries. In other words, these were the guardians of the people *and* their government; they were the original Safeguard System. The question which then arose defied an answer—and still does —Who will guard the guardians?

Does America's infantile reliance on judges provide an answer? Are judges the best defense a democratic society has against government folly, against a government ravage of power? Are they any good at all? If so, what are the limits of their effectiveness?

The problem lies in the so-called independence of the American judiciary, or, perhaps I should say, in its lack of independence. If the system of guardianship, so dependent on judges as guardians, is to work, then judges have to be estranged from other agencies of government. A judge is in the ambivalent position of having to be a government agent (part of the law enforcement process) and simultaneously having to be intellectually free of the government's position in all cases. Unfortunately, it is becoming increasingly clear that many American judges have a difficult time accomplishing this.

A number of American judges consider themselves government officials, and as such they seek to avoid direct and open conflict with other government officials, particularly when those officials are charged with violating the system while enforcing it. Most judges can be far more objective when a government official is charged with graft, since that is a clear violation of role. There is no role conflict. Grafters are solidly outside the law. But when an official is charged with lawlessness in carrying out his duties, that's quite different.

Consider what happens when a defendant calls a policeman a liar. What will a judge do? More than likely, the judge will assume that the policeman is telling the truth. He may be open-minded enough to hear testimony to the contrary, but the burden of proof will be (implicitly) on the defendant.

Why is this so? After all, there is no law that says that a judge must put the burden of proof on a defendant to prove that a policeman is taking undue liberties with the truth. And a judge would be loath to admit such a code exists. But it does. Judges assume policemen are truthful because it is *functional* for them and the system they all serve. The system as it is now established would not function very efficiently if judges didn't believe policemen.

But an efficient system is not necessarily a just one, a good one, or one balanced in favor of individual liberty. And is the latter not the one we Americans say we have? Are not judges supposed to be independent arbiters between parties, whether government is a party or not? A judge who assumes that a policeman (or any government official) has an edge in veracity is not independent. He is a government minister, not a true referee. Indeed, judges depend on their position with the positive policy-making system for personal satisfaction. And that dependence is what makes them inferior guardians' guardians. This is particularly understandable, considering who American judges are, before they ascend to their exalted chairmanship, and what training they *don't* receive.

Almost all American judges were or come to be at least upper-middle-class burghers. They are usually social pillars of their community, with the unquenchable passion for a neoclassical standing order that exists mainly in their nostalgia. Moreover, with remarkably few exceptions, they have dabbled in the political process, with extensive benefit to themselves and their next of kin. It is only due to the favor of the American political system that they rose to judge/priesthood. If they were elected, then they obviously had an intimate and positive experience with politics. If they were appointed, it was through a happy connection with some political official. American judges would seem to have an emotional affinity for the American political system as it stands and for its major product: the law (being lawyers as well). Is this the ideal guardian against government malfeasance? Of course not.

Once they get into office, there are few guidelines to ease them into their role, and particularly as guardians of the guardians. For one thing, there is no training for judges as judges. Of course, there are a few "canons of ethics" they are supposed to learn and abide by, but these are notably vague. American political, governmental, and legal literature contains next to nothing on the need and role of judicial independence—on the critical role of the judge as guardian.

So the whole idea of independence dangles vulnerably, obscurely, and helplessly. The American system pretends that judges are isolated from polities by life tenure, and that this is enough to guarantee independence from other agencies of government. No other official, it is said with a straight face, would try to influence a judge directly. But the whole point is that no one has to. The system coopts the judge so that he tends to think like the other officials anyway.

In truth, in America it is rare that anyone guards the guardians, particularly at the lowest, most important levels of the judiciary. Of course, some judges see this as one of their prime responsibilities, for this book is peppered with instances of where judges were the best or last resort of some citizen against official lawlessness. But they are almost as rare a bird as the whooping crane.

To be fair, when Americans boast of their highly independent judiciary, they usually have in mind the Supreme Court of the United States and its power of judicial review. Such a thought is another flight into fancy, away from the grim truth. Instead of thinking of lower-court judges, who are so critically important in most citizen-government encounters, Americans are conditioned to admire nine high-wire balancing artists, while escaped lions devour parts of the crowd, piecemeal and unnoticed.

Briefly, the Court's "checking power" was usurped by the U.S. Supreme Court in 1803 by John Marshall in a cleverly executed ploy to maintain some Federalist Party presence in national government. The Court overruled one part of the Judiciary Act, passed by Congress in 1789, stating that it was beyond Congress' constitutional authority to give the Court some extra power unauthorized in the Constitution. In denying itself this new and minor power, the Marshall Court cleverly secured for itself a far larger and important power—the power to declare acts of the elected Congress unconstitutional. And the Supreme Court has been doing it ever since. It has become an important part of the American system, almost from its inception, as though it were expressly stated to be so in the Constitution, which it is not. A court system that has the power to overrule acts by other government agencies and does so regularly is far more independent than a court system that lacks that power.

For example, the U.S. Supreme Court tells the President to give up steel mills that have been unconstitutionally nationalized, and the President complies. State supreme courts tell police they have committed an unreasonable search and that the lower courts will not hear the evidence; the suspects go free. They tell administrative agencies that they have acted arbitrarily in denying a permit. The agencies are reversed. They tell lower courts that they have been biased. The lower courts' decisions are overturned.

In other words, all government officials know their action can be reviewed by higher courts in their jurisdiction and reversed because they have violated some higher law, whether the U.S. Constitution, or a state constitution. There can be little doubt that higher court judges exercise this power of judicial review on occasion, and that this is the pinnacle of judicial independence.

Obviously, then, judicial review does curb government lawlessness. But because of the nature of the judiciary, it cannot begin to be a substantial check on some very serious types of government lawlessness.

For example, many people who are victims of government lawlessness cannot or will not go through the rigmarole and expense they associate with the legal system. Further, because many people intuitively feel a lack of judicial independence at the lower levels, they believe, usually with some justification, that the higher courts will probably be inhospitable to their claims of government lawlessness. Third, the high courts cannot even begin to handle many cases of illegal governmental nonaction by judicial review. Fourth, many cases of active governmental lawlessness are not fit for judicial review.

Take a simple case of police brutality in dealing with a suspect. It would take a miracle to generate a reviewable constitutional issue. Even if the lawyer did try to raise it, the case would rest on the lower court's believing the defendant's version of the facts, and we know how most courts react to such disputes. And once the lower courts find on that matter, the high courts almost always abide.

This situation holds true for many serious cases of government lawlessness. The damage—whether physical harm, or harassment, or days or years of illegal detention and valuable resources expended on expensive legal talent—is already done.

So although there is much independence inherent in judicial review, it is a far less potent remedy than is needed, particularly considering the tremendous lack of independence in the lower courts, where it is most needed. Then, too, the Supreme Court may tell the government official to refrain from certain acts, or to do something in a new and constitutional way, but little or nothing will be done.

Finally there is the stultifying effect judicial review has on politics, the one essential ingredient needed to curb government lawlessness. Politics? Yes, politics. For although it is certainly true that the Supreme Court watches the election returns, and is affected by politics, it is also true that the Supreme Court is grandly remote from democratic politics. After all, does the public care about most of the issues up for judicial review? Not much. Every once in a while, the public gets wind of an important issue, but its general ignorance on the subject is exceeded only by its ignorance of the science of moon geology.

Herman Finer, a political scientist, once put it this way: "No doubt lawyers are experts on the construction of legal documents, but the constitution is no ordinary legal document; its spirit can be apprehended by the politicians and the people, who have no need to dispute the judges to act as communal mentors. Everyone is for the rule of law . . . but why must this entail submission to the rule of lawyers?" [5]

Americans have become benumbed to the most important issues of the day; those very issues whose resolutions are the most thrilling to contemplate are largely above and beyond the political system. Government lawlessness, for instance, is certainly a problem of public concern. Should it not be an issue resolved by the political process? Of course it should. But whatever information reaches most of the public filters down in occasional references by political dilettantes, TV talk show moderators, and William F. Buckley.

Is there some compelling reason why a commission or a legion of politically appointed lower-court judges should make such important decisions? Not really. But Americans have become accustomed to the hallucination that their constitutional pains can be relieved only by legal pills.

If only the Supreme Court would do itself in and do America a big favor by overruling *Marbury* v. *Madison,* putting weary "judicial review" to a long-overdue rest. One might as well pin his hopes on the Pentagon's voluntarily requesting a ten-year moratorium on military appropriations.

OMBUDSMANIA

What's worse for America's future is that even its most flaming modernists are such unimaginative dreamers that their worst nightmares fail to awaken even themselves. Those who are thoroughly aware of official lawlessness as The Question and disenchanted with the court system as The Answer turn to a rather faddish solution, one that would further increase America's balance-of-ideas deficit with Europe. They would import still another piece of Scandinavian furniture—the ombudsman's chair.

This renovation by which some of our reformers seek to streamline the American system was adopted in Sweden circa 1809 in its then-new constitution. Oddly enough, there is little information on how the notion was adopted or who was its chief designer. The Swedes, not always complacently neutral, were warring with Russia at the time; and when the constitution emerged behind Swedish lines, there was the ombudsman—though born with another name. It was conceived as an agency to be appointed by the Parliament that had power to supervise judges, government officials, military officers, and just about every civil servant in the pay of the people. Its primary mission was to prosecute those who either acted illegally or neglected their official duties. Though the office has grown in scope and stature since its inception, it remains very much the same armchair conscience.

The ombudsman himself possesses some extraordinary operating powers. He can attend all meetings and deliberations conducted by most government officials, including secret meetings and private judicial conferences. He also has access to classified government information. After investigation, if he decides the government has acted unwisely, unjustly, or illegally, the ombudsman has the power to criticize, reprimand, or prosecute those responsible. Independent even of Parliament itself, he alone (that is, his office) decides on the appropriate action.

Regarding external pressure, Alfred Bexelius, the Swedish civil ombudsman in 1968, recently stated, "Throughout the history of the office there is no evidence whatsoever in the annual reports to support the assumption that undue influences have ever been exerted on the Ombudsman." [6] One can't ask for a better record than that.

Let me relate a refreshing example of how this system works with judges. According to Swedish law, no one under eighteen may be sentenced to jail unless there are "aggravating circumstances." However, one Swedish judge recently sentenced two boys of fifteen and sixteen to some six months in jail. They had been convicted of pilfering some cheap motor scooters. Although the judge did suspend the sentence, the ombudsman saw fit to inquire why the judge meted out such a severe sentence to such young boys, when there was no evidence of any "aggravating circumstances." The judge replied that the boys had needed a warning. The judge was an adherent of an interesting theory of deterrence. But there were still no "aggravating circumstances." No matter how noble the judge's intent, or correct his theory, this was a clear case of a judge disregarding the law. The ombudsman issued a public criticism, for the judge had indeed acted lawlessly. Had the judge not suspended the sentence and put the boys in jail, one would hope the ombudsman would have prosecuted the judge.

The ombudsman idea is a good one, and it is gaining support. Its increasing popularity can be measured in two ways:

the growing appeal of the idea where it is adopted and its rapid proliferation throughout the contemporary world.

In each country where employed, one can almost always detect a trend, emanating from the people themselves, to resort to the ombudsman. This is probably due to increased confidence in the independence and impartiality of the ombudsman, and to the ease with which the process can be started. Such success is a mixed blessing, for ombudsmen nearly everywhere are being swamped. A Swedish government committee recommended, in 1965, that supervision of judges, prison officials, and police should be transferred from the civil ombudsman's office to the ombudsman for military affairs. Bexelius, the civil ombudsman at the time, suggested instead that there be not two different ombudsmen, but three.

Another vote of confidence for the office came in Norway. Although the Socialist government was defeated in 1965 after some twenty years in power, the new Parliament reappointed the same old ombudsman to office for a second term. And in New Zealand, a recent royal commission recommended only one salary increase for a senior civil service position—for the ombudsman.

The cross-cultural spread of the ombudsman is also remarkable. In the sixties alone, the idea was adopted in Britain, Alberta, New Brunswick, and Hawaii. There is substantial agitation for it elsewhere, most notably in America. Some pundits have called the upsurge in American interest for this office "ombudsmania"; by 1967, ombudsman bills had been filed in over half the American states. Ombudsman-type plans were adopted in Michigan and Colorado, but in each of these the ombudsman was part of the executive, rather than the legislative, branch.

The ombudsman concept is so compelling for some Americans that it is even being proposed for quasi-government and nongovernment institutions. For instance, the State University of New York appointed an Ombudsman Committee, comprised of three professors, to hear complaints from students and faculty about the administration.

In 1966, the president of the Michigan Bar Association appointed all seventeen past presidents of that association to serve as ombudsmen. Their job was to hear complaints from members of the bar against current officers of the association.

The idea appeals because it works. How do we know that? Because of the reasonably large number of complaints that ombudsmen themselves find justified. For instance, in New Zealand in 1966, more than half of the complaints received precipitated an ombudsman investigation. And of the investigations made, 16 percent were found to require corrective action. In Tel Aviv, where the ombudsman-style office is attached to the executive, over a thousand complaints were received in its first year, 1966. Of these, the ombudsman's office considered five hundred-plus justified.

OMBUDSMANURE

All this is wonderful. There is substantial merit to the ombudsman, particularly as he cooperates with a rough and tough independent judiciary. A government with both agencies functioning properly would be a government keenly aware of the boundaries of its power. Government lawlessness would face a fair chance of swift and just government retribution.

But the reader is correct in detecting an air of skepticism on my part about the ultimate value of this institution, even with the help of an alert court system.

The ombudsman is less than the most comprehensive solution, and it has some noteworthy disadvantages as well. For example, in all societies in which ombudsmen have appeared, there are inner sancta into which ombudsmen dare not peek, sanctuaries that are off limits even to the supreme watchdog for the people. In Sweden, all high-ranking political ministers are exempt from the ombudsman's prowling, pointing, barking, biting, and retrieving. In other nations, most elected municipal officials are considered immune. Why are these men above the law? Is there something in their character or in the character of their incumbency that makes them less likely to act outside the law? The answer to these questions must be a resounding no. Then how can this sacrosanctity be justified?

The major reason behind the immunity of major elected officials is election itself. If officials act illegally, the argument runs, then this can be converted into a crucial issue in the next election. In other words, the electoral process itself is sufficient to boot the rascals out. Of course this idea is nonsense.

Elections as they now stand are hardly the place to air grievances of official anarchy. It would be next to impossible to produce evidence of the lawlessness. While ombudsmen in some countries can subpoena even supersecret documents, no candidate for elected office in any country has such a right today. Whatever changes could be made in these rules would probably be treated by most of the electorate as an electoral tactic.

Perhaps if we gave the party out of power a right to investigate or cause an impartial investigation to be made, this might go a long way to reform the election process and make it sufficient to supplement the ombudsman as a check on high, exempt, elected officials. But official incumbents would probably favor ombudsman scrutiny over that of an electoral opponent. And there is small hope for either as things stand now.

So this is a serious shortcoming to the ombudsman as a panacea for American government lawlessness, unless American ombudsmen were allowed entry into the Supreme Courts, the Congress, the Presidency, the governors' rooms, etc. And what do you think is the likelihood of that?

But the fatal flaw in ombudsmanship as that trade is currently plied is that the ombudsman is just one more step in the bureaucratization of society. Isn't the ombudsman but another facet of the philosophy that promotes government as the omnipotent, the omniscient, and omnibus dispenser of justice? The ombudsman is just another clever device to seduce people into the overprotective clutches of government as the surrogate parent, firm but compassionate. This philosophy beatifies King Solomon, but ignores King Sadim, whose touch turned gold to manure.

The philosophers and prophets of ombudsmania also point out the importance of the ombudsman for democracy. Just the reverse is true. In no society is the ombudsman elected by the people. It is not an office for which men run. It is always an office that is filled by appointment, either by the legislature or by the executive. It may well be independent and impartial, but it is always well beyond democratic—popular—politics. This is not to say that the ombudsman idea and its supporters are antidemocratic. But up to now, the office of ombudsman has certainly been undemocratic.

Whether judge or ombudsman, then, the power to check government lawlessness floats in pure and celestial isolation, far above the madding crowd.

The ombudsman is nothing more or less than an aristocrat in democrat's clothing. To support the ombudsman concept is to opt for the sterilization of the people as direct participants in their own rule. And, in the end, why should such an office be required to help the people help themselves against government lawlessness? Constitutional issues are not so obscure that the people cannot themselves root out those men who profane their own oaths of office, the duly promulgated laws of their government, and the supreme contract between government and the people. The ombudsman is just another, more sophisticated, way to rob the people of involvement in the most crucial issues in the system that menaces them.

So, America has been thinking about stopping government anarchy, a little bit here, and a little bit there. It places much faith in helter-skelter reforms of various institutions, as well as on the courts, who are supposed to play Big Daddy. Those who see the danger in relying on the courts place their hopes in the ombudsmen. But the unrelated reforms are band-aids and the judges and ombudsmen, first aid. Meanwhile the patient is in critical condition.

What is needed for such a battered body politic is complete rehabilitation.

9

The

POGONOGO Alternative

> If it is bad garbage, it will quickly rot, if it is good garbage it will help transform the pile into a shrine of holiness.
>
> —*Abbie Hoffman*

What must be done in America is twofold. First, federal and some local government anarchy laws must be passed. Then, an extensive *countergovernment* (NOGO) must be founded. This countergovernment's exclusive role must be to check the positive government. The countergovernment, or antigovernment, must be elected, must have access to all levels and offices of government, and must not be denied access to any documents or conferences. Its sole purpose is to probe, evaluate, and if necessary, condemn, government officials charged with disregarding the law of the land.

This is the only sure way we can compel government to adhere to the law. This is the only way we can reverse the apparently relentless trend toward a government beyond law that has become the American political tragedy of the twentieth century. It is the only way to shrivel official anarchy to minute proportions, to make it of no moment.

Do we need a "government anarchy law?" Isn't there a glut of laws that cover most of the abuses described above? Aren't there many other living laws, easily expandable to include the remaining malconduct of government officials? The answer to all of these questions is yes—despite the apparent inconsistency.

There are *many* laws already on the books, aimed directly at the government official, that provide potential legal remedy for government abuse of office. "Abuse of process" and "false imprisonment," for example, are laws found here and there which prohibit law enforcement officers from exercising their power over the criminal process to serve their own personal sense of rectitude. And, of course, the whole criminal code is applicable against any number of government officers who commit any number of evils. Assault and battery, kidnaping, crossing state lines to incite riots, conspiracy, or depriving citizens of their civil rights—all of these charges can be pinned onto many government vestments for many such acts done regularly. So why do we need a "government anarchy law?" What could it accomplish?

All these laws, though they constitute the framework of a system that could diminish official anarchy, fail to show much life. They may be there, waiting to spring into action, but there is little hope they will ever receive the attention they so richly deserve. They are like Chiang's army: billions of dollars' worth of equipment, but an underwhelming desire to use it.

How often are government officials indicted on any such charges? When it happens, it is an event that gobbles up front-page space with the voraciousness of killer tornadoes.

Moreover, the equipment looks obsolete. It is still usable, but it seems to be too little, too late. Passage of a "government anarchy act" would be an important first step in streamlining the legal code as it pertains to government anarchy. It would be a formal warning to government that the political system at last reflects public concern over the spread of government lawlessness. Furthermore, since it would apply specifically to officials, it would make *government* kidnaping, *government* assault and battery, *government* conspiracy, *government* perjury, distinguishable general felonies—which in fact they are.

Actually, we should consider the possibility of making the penalties even harsher than their civilian equivalents, since there are the added elements of violation of public trust and desecration of a sacred institution, and because the façade of authority lulls people into lowering their natural defenses. In other words, people are more vulnerable to damage and outrage by this crime, and the sentences should be extra stiff ones with little room for judicial discretion to commute or water them down.

What would be the most appropriate jurisdiction for this

act? Since official anarchy knows no political bounds in America —since it breeds at all levels of government, from the marble halls of Congress to the termite magistracy of West Pachoochnik —an act to stop it needs passage at multiple levels, federal and state in particular. In order to promote standardization, we should encourage a "uniform government anarchy act" covering the whole range of state and local abuses. Since the federal government is far from immune from the disease, Congress must take up its own cudgels and include federal officials as well as local and state officials who might do their illegal thing across state or national boundaries.

So much for the substantive legal tools. This would be easy enough to design (though getting it passed would be something else). A sample follows:

THE GOVERNMENT ANARCHY LAW

(1) Any government official who, in the performance of his duties, knowingly and wilfully violates any provision or provisions of the federal Constitution, his own state constitution, any act of Congress or of his state or local legislature, any court order or Supreme Court decision, any regulation of his own agency, or violates the sworn requirements of his oath of office, is guilty of government anarchy, and shall be subject to the penalties set forth hereunder.

The penalties for government anarchy shall be commensurate with those of similar felonies and misdemeanors committed by private citizens, except that those penalties, other than the maximum, shall be greater by 25 percent. Furthermore, conviction of government anarchy shall result in immediate removal of the officeholder from his official position and shall bar him for life from all other official positions.

(a) Government anarchy directly resulting in death shall be punishable by life imprisonment.

(b) Government anarchy resulting in aggravated or permanent serious physical or psychological injury shall be punishable as crimes of aggravated assault and battery, mayhem, and/or attempted homicide.

(c) Government anarchy resulting in less than aggravated and temporary physical or psychological injury shall be punishable as crimes of simple assault and battery and/or disturbing the peace.

(d) Government anarchy resulting in detention of a person against his will shall be punishable as the crime of kidnaping.

(e) Government anarchy resulting in intrusions on a private citizen's right to enjoy his own personal or real property shall be punishable as the crime of criminal trespass.

(f) Government anarchy resulting in damage or destruction of personal or real property shall be punishable as the crime of arson.

(2) It shall be a felony to conspire to commit government anarchy.

(3) Any government official who attempts to impede a citizen or official of the countergovernment trying to deter or make an arrest for acts of government anarchy shall be guilty of the crime of interference with the enforcement of the government anarchy act. If done with knowledge of the act of government anarchy, it shall be punishable as the crime of impeding the administration of justice.

(4) (a) Any government official who wilfully attempts to withhold or disguise any information of the commission of acts of government anarchy, committed by himself or any other government official, is guilty of the crime of aiding and abetting government anarchy, and shall be punished as a co-conspirator.

(b) Any government official who deliberately misleads any medium of public communication about the truth of governmental operations, whether they be acts of government anarchy or not, shall be guilty of the crime of unlawful information manipulation, which shall be punishable as the crime of criminal libel.

POGO AND NOGO

It seems pretty obvious, though, that no amount of modernizing our laws will get our presently constituted government off its collective seat of power to enforce them vigorously. Even when the laws are clear about government anarchy, and even when it would seem that government has no option but to be strict in its enforcement, it lets us down.

Some analogies in the life sciences may be useful in giving us a hint as to how we might better protect our ailing body politic. What we know about antibodies, for example, might be of some help to us. An antibody, as the reader might know, is matter generated by the body to check and repulse the advance of an alien body. Whenever our bodily system is disrupted from normal, healthy functioning, it creates antimatter able to combat and, hopefully, defeat the unwelcome organism.

By analogy, official anarchy is a toxic disrupter and potential destroyer of our political system. What was thought at first to be a superficial problem is obviously the surface symptom of a deep infection. The body by itself has not yet come up with an effective antibody to engage and defeat it. It is for science—modern political science—to ponder what that antibody might be and then to persuade society to test the remedy as quickly as possible. It seems clear that *something* has to be added to the system. For once, some grafting might be in the public interest.

My own feeling right now is that the most productive antibody would be a comprehensive antigovernment or countergovernment. The best way to separate the powers of modern government would be to constitute an entirely new government apart from, but the mirror image of, the positive government. It would be like institutionalizing and empowering the loyal opposition or shadow government of England. It would officially pit one government faction against another in terms of carrying out the limited, delegated powers of each faction.

The solitary object of antigovernment would be to monitor

the exercise of power by those in positive government, that is, the policymaking positive government, which we could call POGO. Since the primary function of the new countergovernment is *negative,* and since it will be in business to keep POGO on the straight and narrow, I propose that we call the new counteragencies Negative Ortho-Government, or NOGO.

Of course, this proposal defies all principles of parsimony and all unorthodoxies and revisionisms of pure and not so pure Marxism. It would complicate our government apparatus immeasurably and might be thought to admit to the permanent and eternal staying power of government. Instead of withering away, government would flourish. We'd have more government officials than ever, all of whom would be far more contentious than ever—but at least with each other. What better way to keep them occupied and off the streets?

The most important single feature of NOGO would be that it would be elected by the people. Instead of electing someone we call an ombudsman, we would elect the Nogopresident or Nogogovernor or Nogochief. In effect, he would be a super-ombudsman, the overall coordinator of all NOGO goings-on. In another sense, he would be the chief counteradministrator, since there would be very few legislative proposals that would concern him. In fact, the only legislative functions of NOGO would be to recommend additions, alterations, or deletions to the government anarchy law. The major job of the NOGO administration would be to implement the government anarchy law as written at the time.

There would be a judiciary, or I should say a counterjudiciary, whose exclusive function would be to try cases against government officials accused and indicted as government anarchists. The judges on this court could be, as in some regular American judiciaries, elected by the people after extensive campaigning. In order to keep them independent of the government and the people—and other Nogopersons as well—once elected, they should be in for life. Their role, as should be clear by now, would be an impartial and independent judgment of charges levied against POGO.

The main body of NOGO would be a bank of divisions and bureaus corresponding to those various agencies of POGO covered earlier. Special divisions could be set up for evaluating, investigating, and reevaluating reports and complaints of anarchy against police, the asylums, the bureaucracy, the courts, the prosecutor's office, and state and local elected officials, among others.

With the guaranteed independence and election of Nogojudges, there would be no need to elect the top officers of each of these divisions just as there is no need to elect the Cabinet or chief ministers in all contemporary democracies. The appointment of the chiefs of these antidivisions would be the responsibility of the Nogopresident or Counterpresident (COP) or whatever we call him. As a candidate for this office, he might announce his intentions to fill these lesser posts with major critics or victims of official anarchy, in order to put his opponent (or POGO officials) on the spot. For instance, a challenger for Nogopresident might claim the incumbent was "soft" on anarchy and threaten to appoint Ralph Nader as chief of the NOGObureaucrat Bureau. So it might go.

The reader may be skeptical about how NOGO would accumulate evidence on government anarchy, since POGO personnel might develop an even more efficient code of silence to thwart their enemies in NOGO. POGO is pretty secretive nowadays, freedom of information acts notwithstanding. Such heavy skepticism probably persists because we fail to see how easy it would be to use POGO's past and present ingenuity (and lawlessness) against itself in the future. After all, POGO has developed a brilliant system of spying on private citizens and—occasionally—on itself too, using everything from electronic olives to laser beams in its compulsive obsession for the Hidden Truth.

So in addition to giving NOGO free access to documents

and meetings, formal and informal, there seems to be no good reason to let all the spy apparatus and snooping techniques gather dust. Indeed, they can now be put to their proper use, eavesdropping on POGO in an authorized and legal fashion by the dedicated men and women of NOGO. Being on the job twenty-four hours a day, the officials of POGO should be open to public view, particularly if there may be a reasonable suspicion of illegal behavior on their part. So NOGO must gain expertise in bugging the Pentagon, using spike-mikes in mashies to underhear golf-course chatter by POGO's, monitoring hidden closed-circuit TV in police stations, police cars, and the like. The possibilities can boggle the imagination even of political science fiction writers.

"Moderation" being the motto of NOGO, responsible NOGO cops would, of course, have to apply for spy warrants and equipment issues from NOGO judges, who could only grant them for "probable cause."

Is this fighting evil with evil? Is it thinking that two wrongs make a right? It certainly isn't. Those who choose to work within the legal framework of POGO have nothing to fear if they are innocent. Since they made the conscious, free choice to enter public service, their every action should be subject to public scrutiny anyway. We want government to know government is in the public eye. We want our citizens to know *they* aren't!

As for NOGO elections and the electorate, there are several options. Everyone is to be allowed to vote for both POGO and NOGO candidates. There would be two separate ballots. On one ballot, each citizen could choose among those to be responsible for positive legislation and administration. On the second, he could choose among those who claim that more or less (or special types of) government anarchy must be curbed, or that the current NOGO is working too hard and that we need less negativism. Another option would be to let the electorate divide itself into an electorate and counterelectorate, thereby publicizing the relative extent of public concern over positive and negative government's actions over the past years of incumbency. In either event, the very charter of government would be a major election issue. Vigorous accounting would have to be done at regular intervals. Campaigns would be a far sight more interesting and meaningful than they are these days.

How could we make sure that NOGO would be well enough financed to do its job? After all, if POGO wanted to get NOGO off its back, it could manipulate the purse strings in such a way as to seriously cripple its operations. It cannot be left to POGO to appropriate the necessary monies. And it would be ridiculous to fix precise constitutional amounts of expenditure, for there may be greater or lesser needs for countergovernment at different times. So what can be done?

What we need to remember is that there probably is a high correlation between the soaring rate of official anarchy these days and the great expansion of positive government at all levels. POGO already finances its expanding anarchistic elements, as well as its burgeoning legitimate functions. Consequently, in order to assure sufficient finances for countergovernment activities, all we need do is, constitutionally, compel positive government to allocate an extra 50 or 25 or 33⅓ percent of its own expenditures to NOGO. In figuring out its annual budget, positive government must take into account its constitutional obligation to spend a fixed extra percentage of its own expenditures annually on its own shadow.

Assuming that POGO is not about to cut its own throat fiscally, and that Parkinson's Law will continue to work even in the Era of POGONOGO, this would guarantee the necessary working funds, at least at the beginning, for the adequate functioning of Negative Ortho-Government. And, as POGO agencies bloom in number and function, so will their counterparts. If POGO cuts back in its own legitimate affairs (and thus cuts back on the appropriations for NOGO), the amount of official anarchy would decrease anyway—which is the primary goal of our new system.

What about those official anarchists who are tried and convicted? Are they to languish in POGO's prisons after they are sentenced to some period of confinement? At least at the birth of the new NOGO faction, there should be special prison official-anarchist compounds for wayward prison officials. However, we should keep in mind the possibility of expanding this to general official-anarchist compounds, should the regular prison system be less than fair to all kinds of government anarchists.

These suggestions may raise a totally new question in political philosophy, namely, Who will guard the guardians' guardians? This is a clear new step in an infinite regression. But though the question is without philosophical answer, there are many practical points raised by the solution that have the virtue of skirting the issue.

First, my solution makes clear that the current traditional solutions—and their inevitable revisions and extensions—are inadequate and are bound, practically by definition, to malfunction. This new proposal is not anti-American or un-American, antidemocratic or undemocratic. It is simply strange. It has the obvious merit that it would radically curtail if not eliminate official anarchy in America, at least among those in POGO.

My second point is that, practically speaking, it would not result in other malfunctions that seem apparent. NOGO personnel might nurse political grudges, and abuse their role requirement for objectivity, and therefore hassle or threaten or persecute perfectly righteous government officials. Enough of this might make antigovernment more antimatter rather than antibody, and annihilate the entire system. If NOGO became too negative for political or personal reasons, no sane man would seek POGO office for fear that he would be political-prisoner fodder at worst, or too hamstrung by NOGO to be able to do that which he feels is within his authority, and essential to his duty, to do. How can I guarantee that this would not happen? I cannot—theoretically.

I can only suggest, practically, that the unanswerability of the question of who will guard the guardians, and the fact that many of them act beyond their power, has not stopped many positive governments from doing a fair to good job up to now. But the philosophical and empirical unanswerability of the guardians question has made the risk of being a plain and ordinary citizen very great at times, particularly when the citizenry has spoken up for some important changes in the system.

Perhaps NOGO would make the positive running of government more frustrating and dangerous and lower the degree and quality of government output in some regards. But is that all bad? It might make people who wanted to play POGO roles think twice about it, particularly when the underlying reasons for their eagerness for high office are less than the noble ones they rationalize and publicize.

Yes, POGO people would be in a more perilous position. But to that I might raise a loud Hurrah! Perhaps it would be better for the rulers to live more perilously in society than the ruled. After all, they chose to seek power, and the use of all power is risky. We have let our rulers underestimate the high tension of political power. Now is the time to think about setting them on the right track.

In the words of the Moody Blues:

> Time is now to spread your voice
> Time's to come there'll be no choice.

Am I serious about all this? Yes, but no. "Yes," because we have seen all governmental systems, and particularly our own, tip dangerously in favor of unlimited government. I seriously believe that my proposition is the only logical way to balance our system properly. The POGONOGO Alternative is the purest solution to the dilemma; it is not the paragon of virtue, but there is great virtue in the paragon. Although it raises a new philosophical inquiry—or, rather, a new version of an ancient one—it does furnish an answer to the old one simultaneously. As a matter of fact, the POGONOGO model would probably diminish government anarchy substantially, while generating only a much smaller degree of new official mis- and malconduct. It seems to me that the net gain would readily justify the institution of the strange system I have outlined.

The "no" refers to the pragmatic feasibility of such a system in form, as well as in name. There does not seem to me to be a ghost of a chance that such a system could ever find ample popular support to win its place in this nation's political sun.

So that leaves me with the task of describing just what I think would be most feasible and most consistent with the ideal.

The components of this feasible system would be as follows: (1) an elected federal ombudsman, with (2) branch and agency functional departments (e.g., police, military, judicial, legislative), each having (3) unlimited access to all respective governmental activities, sessions, meetings, hearings, and documents, and (4) each having license to employ all electronic data discovery devices devisable (but only to ensure that government is kept at legal bay).

It would also be highly desirable to establish a special court (since a NOGO judiciary seems unlikely) like the current U.S. Court of Claims, which entertains only cases against the government. Other federal judges often hear the government's prosecution of cases against private interests. The extraordinary Government Anarchy Court could be the exclusive forum of original jurisdiction for the U.S. ombudsman, when he decides that the judicial remedy is the last resort against the government in a specific case. And it would relieve positive-government judges of the difficult (and sometimes irreconcilable) burden of trying to remain impartial and independent in cases against other positive-government agents. A special government anarchy type of judge would be socialized, first, foremost, and exclusively to recognize that his sole mission is to dampen governmental overzealousness that laps over into the realm of the illegal and/or unconstitutional.

I may be a dreamer in believing that it is possible for the American system to adopt or adapt these notions in the not too distant future. It is a strange bag of new structures: an immensely potent federal ombudsman, along with a Government Anarchy Court and a special law (the government anarchy law). What all this adds up to is a comprehensive civilian review board of all governmental activities.

Admittedly, this set-up could never become a reality unless droves of Americans awaken to the frightening awareness that governmental excess of power is easily one of the most serious problems that could confront any society and that it has become a particularly deadly threat to the open character of our own. The government-negative function has been talked about—abstractly—in America from even before the inception of the federal Constitution in 1787. Many partial solutions have been suggested, tested, patched, discarded, and disregarded. The wholesale governmental anarchy that has pervaded our history has, thanks largely to technology, only recently allowed government to go much too far, and has given the American people a glimpse of the horrendous scenario of what may yet come.

The best time is now—to think seriously about starting anew, to sculpt the inspiration of limited government, very limited government, into the work of political art it can still be. The fact that this can best be done by means of an ostensible paradox, through more government, is a contradiction only on the surface. One can adhere to the tenets of antigovernmentalism without being an anarchist. For at a deeper level of reality, the negative reverses the superficial, its mirror reflection. A negative government, properly organized and socialized, is not more government. It is no more poisonous to a body than any vaccine or any antitoxin would be, if the initial poison were not so lethal in the first place. And remember that it takes a diamond to cut a diamond.

Finally, we are into the Age of Antibodies. In late 1971, Americans witnessed the founding of the first anticorporation, established to wage business against illegal or dangerous activities of other corporations. It is one way in which business-oriented types can serve the public. Similarly, new public-interest law firms are antisystem in that they practice law not for profit, but for the common weal.

Antigovernment can be the way anti-government-oriented types can advance the public good for its own sake. The building blocks already exist, from consumer protection bureaus to limited-jurisdiction ombudsmen. POGONOGO puts them together, along with a few additions, and some nuts and bolts. Like most innovations, it's new but not all new.

As my mother was fond of saying, "They laughed at Fulton."

Notes

1. GOVERNMENT ANARCHY—NOT JUST ANOTHER PROBLEM

1. Georgie Anne Geyra and Keyes Beech, "A Revolution Against Hypocrisy," *Honolulu Star-Bulletin*, December 2, 1970, p. A-23. (One in a series of ten articles.)
2. Ernest Jerome Hopkins, *Our Lawless Police* (New York, Viking, 1931), p. 13.

3. POLICE ANARCHY

1. The director of the Performance Group is Richard Schechner, a well-known proponent and ideologue of guerrilla theater. The Performance Group is best known to date for its productions of *Dionysius 69* (1969) and *Commune* (1970–71).
2. Directed by Alec Rubin.
3. F. K. Heussenstamm, "Bumper Stickers and the Cops," *Trans/Action*, February 1971, pp. 32–33.
4. *Trans/Action*, July-August 1968, pp. 10–20.
5. See Staff Report No. 10 of the National Commission on the Causes and Prevention of Violence (Washington, D.C., Government Printing Office), p. 382.
6. "Perspective," *Los Angeles Times*, March 7, 1971.
7. J. Anthony Lukas, "Boston Police Raid Investigated," *New York Times*, May 15, 1970, pp. 1, 20.
8. *Newsweek*, March 1, 1971, p. 69.
9. "War Foes Here Attacked by Construction Workers," *New York Times*, May 9, 1970, p. 10.
10. "Whites in Chicago Continue Protest," *New York Times*, September 27, 1969.

11. "Police Scuffle with Building Job Marchers," *Los Angeles Times,* August 27, 1969, p. 16.
12. *Time,* June 22, 1970, p. 16.
13. *Newsweek,* November 9, 1970, p. 21.
14. William W. Turner, *The Police Establishment* (New York, Putnam, 1968), p. 18.
15. See *Law and Order Reconsidered* (Washington, D.C., Government Printing Office, 1969), p. 292.
16. *Escobedo v. Illinois,* 378 U.S. 478 (1964).
17. *Miranda v. Arizona,* 384 U.S. 436 (1966).
18. Michael Wald *et al.,* "Interrogations in New Haven: The Impact of Miranda," *Yale Law Journal,* 1967, pp. 1521–1648.
19. *Police Power* (New York, Pantheon, 1969).

4. THE MILITARY AND OTHER ASYLUMS

1. "CONUS Intelligence: The Army Watches Civilian Politics," *I. F. Stone's Washington Monthly,* January 1970, p. 5.
2. "Army Spied on 18,000 Civilians in 2-Year Operation," *New York Times,* January 18, 1971, p. 1.
3. "Persons of Interest," *Life,* March 26, 1971, p. 21.
4. *New York Times,* January 11, 1971, p. 31.
5. Governor's Select Commission, *Report for Action,* Conclusion No. 8.
6. Telford Taylor, *Nuremberg and Vietnam* (Chicago, Quadrangle Books, 1970), pp. 144–45.
7. Erving Goffman, *Asylums* (Chicago, Aldine, 1961).
8. *Military Justice Is to Justice as Military Music Is to Music* (New York, Random House, 1970).
9. See Karl Purnell, "The Army's Kangaroo Courts," *Nation,* April 7, 1969, pp. 432–34.
10. See "The Hog-Tied Brig Rats of Camp Pendleton," *Life,* October 10, 1969, pp. 32–37.
11. R. Joe Pierpoint, "Torture at Fort Dix," *New Politics,* April, 1968, pp. 5–14.
12. *Time,* February 21, 1969, pp. 17–18.
13. Sara Harris, *Hellhole* (New York, Dutton, 1967).
14. *Ibid.,* p. 16.
15. *Ibid.,* p. 27.
16. With Joe Hyams, *Accomplices to the Crime* (New York, Grove, 1969), p. 7.

17. *Ibid.*, pp. 188–89.
18. *Village Voice*, June 5, 1969, p. 44.
19. "Scandal in Virginia," *Newsweek*, November 15, 1971, p. 39.
20. *West Virginia* ex rel. *Pingley v. Coiner*, Circuit Court of Randolph County, May 6, 1971.
21. Distributed by Grove Press Films, New York City.
22. Jerry Farber, *The Student as Nigger* (North Hollywood, Contact Books, 1969).

5. BUREAUCRATIC ANARCHY

1. "Poverty, Injustice, and the Welfare State," *Nation*, February 28, 1966.
2. Michael B. Rosen, "Tenants' Rights in Public Housing," *Housing for the Poor: Rights and Remedies*, Project on Social Welfare Law, New York University Law School, Supplement No. 1 (1967), p. 168.
3. *Chicago Daily Law Bulletin*, April 26, 1968, pp. 10–11.
4. Committee for Efficiency in Government, Report, 1970, p. 11.
5. *Berger v. U.S.*, 295 U.S. 78, 88 (1935).
6. *Newsweek*, March 8, 1971, p. 32.
7. *Miller v. Pate*, 386 U.S. 1 (1967).
8. *Giles v. Maryland*, 386 U.S. 66 (1967).
9. *Giles v. Maryland*, 386 U.S., 98, 99.
10. *New York Times*, January 16, 1971, pp. 1, 23.
11. From the transcript of the opinion by Judge Jerry Pacht, Superior Court of California, Los Angeles, 1969.
12. *New York Times*, September 15, 1970, p. 56.
13. *Ibid.*, January 20, 1970.
14. *Ibid.*, December 6, 1969, p. 113.
15. See Omar Garrison, *Spy Government* (New York, Lyle Stuart, 1967).

6. JUDICIAL ANARCHY

1. New York, David McKay, 1971.
2. *Ibid.*, p. 7.
3. *Ibid.*, p. 10.
4. *Brown v. Board of Education*, 347 U.S. 438 (1954).
5. Staff Report No. 3 of the National Commission on the Causes and Prevention of Violence (Washington, D.C., Government Printing Office, 1969).

6. *Ibid.*, p. 228.
7. *New York Times,* January 12, 1971, p. 18.
8. Herbert L. Packer, "The Conspiracy Weapon," *New York Review of Books* book *Trials of the Resistance* (New York, Vintage Books, 1970), p. 183.
9. *Ibid.*, pp. 130–31.
10. Jessica Mitford, *The Trial of Dr. Spock* (New York, Knopf, 1969), pp. 155–56.
11. See Joel Grossman and Kenneth Dolbeare, "LeRoi Jones in Newark," in Theodore L. Becker, ed., *Political Trials* (Indianapolis, Bobbs Merrill, 1971).
12. *Ibid.*, p. 235.
13. *Ibid.*, p. 232.
14. *Ibid.*, p. 245.
15. *Ibid.*
16. *Ibid.*, p. 232.
17. LeRoi Jones, "Black People," *Evergreen Review,* December 1967.
18. Stephen Schneck, "LeRoi Jones on Politics and Policemen . . . ," *Ramparts,* June 29, 1968, pp. 14–19.
19. *Newsweek,* January 15, 1968, p. 24.
20. *New York Times,* January 5, 1968.
21. *New Jersey v. Jones* et al., 104, N.J. Supr. 57 (1968).
22. Transcript, pp. A77–A78.
23. Transcript, pp. A82–A83.
24. The transcript for the contempt citation can be found in the *New York Review of Books,* December 4, 1967, pp. 35–50. All of the following excerpts on the contempt citation are from that source.
25. *New York Times,* February 1, 1970, p. E–12.
26. Tom Hayden, *Trial* (New York, Holt, Rinehart & Winston, 1971), pp. 58–62.
27. New York, Columbia University Press, 1963.

7. LOCAL OFFICIAL ANARCHY

1. *New York Times,* November 29, 1969, p. 68.
2. "Post Town Upset by Antiwar G.I.s," *New York Times,* November 9, 1969, p. 30.
3. Sparling Report, p. 23.

4. *Ibid.*, p. 18.
5. *Ibid.*, p. 29.
6. *Ibid.*, p. 54.
7. *Ibid.*, p. 55.
8. In re *Debs*, 158 U.S. 564 (1895).
9. *New York Post*, April 6, 1970.
10. *New York Times*, April 14, 1970, p. 37.
11. New York, Pantheon, 1965.
12. *Ibid.*, p. 37.
13. *Southern Justice*, p. 65.
14. *Ibid.*, p. 65.
15. *U.S. v. Louisiana*, 225 F. Supp., at p. 381.
16. Erwin N. Griswold, *Law and Lawyers in the United States: The Common Law Under Stress* (London: Stevens, 1964), p. 125.
17. *Negroes, Ballots and Judges* (University of Alabama Press, 1968), p. 21.
18. Harold Norris, "Official Disobedience Plus Civil Disorder," *Journal of Urban Law*, Vol. 46 (1969), p. 226.
19. *Ibid.*, p. 105.
20. *Cox v. Louisiana*, 368 U.S. 157 (1965).
21. *Ibid.*, p. 139.
22. See *Hamilton v. Alabama*, 376 U.S. 650 (1964).
23. "Mondale Visits South, Finds Bias Unchecked," *Los Angeles Times*, July 26, 1970, p. 9.
24. *Ibid.*
25. *Ibid.*
26. *Newsweek*, April 5, 1971, p. 86.

8. First Aid Is Little Help

1. *New York Times*, November 19, 1969, p. 57.
2. *Focus/Midwest*, Vol. 6, No. 40, p. 15.
3. William A. Westley, "The Use and Misuse of Violence by Police," abridged and edited by Ritchie P. Lowry and Robert P. Lankin, *Sociology: The Science of Society* (New York, Scribner, 1969), pp. 538–39.
4. "Study Questions Handling of Police Misconduct," *New York Times*, November 20, 1970, pp. 1, 4.

5. *The Theory and Practice of Modern Government* (New York, Holt, Rinehart & Winston, rev. ed., 1949), p. 151.
6. Alfred Bexelius, Sweden's Ombudsman for Civil Affairs, in his article "The Ombudsman for Civil Affairs," in Donald C. Rowat, ed., *The Ombudsman* (London, George Allen and Unwin, 1968), p. 25.